THE BORDERS OF BAPTISM

THEOPOLITICAL VISIONS

SERIES EDITORS:

Thomas Heilke
D. Stephen Long
and C. C. Pecknold

Theopolitical Visions seeks to open up new vistas on public life, hosting fresh conversations between theology and political theory. This series assembles writers who wish to revive theopolitical imagination for the sake of our common good.

Theopolitical Visions hopes to re-source modern imaginations with those ancient traditions in which political theorists were often also theologians. Whether it was Jeremiah's prophetic vision of exiles "seeking the peace of the city," Plato's illuminations on piety and the civic virtues in the Republic, St. Paul's call to "a common life worthy of the Gospel," St. Augustine's beatific vision of the City of God, or the gothic heights of medieval political theology, much of Western thought has found it necessary to think theologically about politics, and to think politically about theology. This series is founded in the hope that the renewal of such mutual illumination might make a genuine contribution to the peace of our cities.

FORTHCOMING VOLUMES:

John C. Nugent
The Politics of YHWH: John Howard Yoder, the Old Testament, and Social Ethics

Peter J. Leithart
Empire: A Biblical and Augustinian Analysis

Braden P. Anderson
Chosen Nation: Scripture, Theopolitics, and the Project of National Identity

The Borders of
BAPTISM

Identities, Allegiances,

and the Church

MICHAEL L. BUDDE

CASCADE *Books* · Eugene, Oregon

THE BORDERS OF BAPTISM
Identities, Allegiances, and the Church

Theopolitical Visions 11

Cascade Books
An Imprint of Wipf and Stock Publishers
199 W. 8th Ave., Suite 3
Eugene, OR 97401

www.wipfandstock.com

ISBN 13: 978-1-61097-135-5

Cataloging-in-Publication data:

Budde, Michael L.

    The borders of baptism : identities, allegiances, and the church / Michael L. Budde.

    viii + 196 p. ; 23 cm. — Includes bibliographical references.

    Thepolitical Visions 11

    ISBN 13: 978-1-61097-135-5

    1. Baptism. 2. Political theology. 3. Religion and politics. I. Title. II. Series.

BT83.59 .B83 2011

Manufactured in the U.S.A.

To Terri, who teaches me what it means to be a Christian.

Contents

Contents

PART I

Introductory Concepts on Ecclesial Solidarity

CHAPTER 1

Ad Extra:
Ecclesial Solidarity and Other Allegiances

This book outlines an important concept—what I call "ecclesial solidarity"—that must be reclaimed and deepened if the Christian Church is to continue serving the Kingdom of God in our day. By "ecclesial solidarity" I mean the conviction that "being a Christian" is one's primary and formative loyalty, the one that contextualizes and defines the legitimacy of other claimants on allegiance and conscience—those of class, nationality, and state, for example.

Ecclesial solidarity means that the welfare of one's brothers and sisters in Christ makes special claims on one's affections, resources, and priorities. It means that the unity of the churches in visible and tangible ways is a key expression of Christian conviction and vocation, even in the face of centrifugal pressures and the demands of lesser, more partial communities and ideologies. It means that processes of Christian discernment and worship cross the divides of patriotism and other types of tribalism, making one's coreligionists the "to whom" we owe service, love and mutual support.

Ecclesial solidarity is not in conflict with the love and service that Christians owe their proximate neighbors, those with whom they live and work and interact on a regular basis. Taking care of one's non-local relatives need not, after all, invariably oppress one's next-door neighbors or work colleagues. It does, however, prohibit Christians from harming their non-local relatives on the assumption that one's neighbors always and inevitably present morally determinative claims on Christian allegiance, priorities, and actions.

When Christians take ecclesial solidarity as their starting point for discernment—political, economic, liturgical, and otherwise—it makes them members of a community broader than the largest nation-state, more pluralistic than any culture in the world, more deeply rooted in the lives of the poor and marginalized than any revolutionary movement, more capable of exemplifying the notion of "E pluribus unum" than any empire past, present, or future. Seeing oneself as a member of the world-wide body of Christ invites communities to join their local stories to other stories of sin and redemption, sacrifice and martyrdom, rebellion and forgiveness unlike any other on offer via allegiance to one's tribe, gendered movements, or class fragment.

Ecclesial solidarity is not a bogus cosmopolitanism that seeks to escape the local and the particular by recourse to an abstract or idealized "world citizenship." It is emphatically not part of a putative "clash of civilizations," drawing Christians together in order to wage war (literal or otherwise) against Muslims, Hindus, or secularists. It is not a transnational political party or diaspora political force, orchestrating political takeovers or seeking power in various national governments. Ecclesial solidarity is not a statement that God loves Christians more than other people, that Christians are better than other people, or that God only works through the Christian community.

Properly conceived and practiced, ecclesial solidarity is not a straightjacketed homogenization of faith, nor an imposition of power that denies the integrity of the local church. To the contrary, the absence of ecclesial solidarity across national, ethnic, and other divides has allowed pathologies to fester within churches north and south; the integrity and mission of the churches require the local and universal to exist in a dialectical interplay of creativity and correction.

The fallout from the existing subordination of Christianity to other allegiances, loyalties, and identities is widespread, scandalous, and lethal. That it is no longer noteworthy nor even noticed—when Christians kill one another in service to the claims of state, ethnicity, or ideology—itself is the most damning indictment of Christianity in the modern era. How can Christians be good news to the world, in what ways can they presume to be a foretaste of the peaceful recuperation of creation promised by God, when their slaughter of one another is so routine as to be beneath comment? World War I is described as interstate rivalry run amok, not the industrial butchering by Christians of one another; Rwanda symbolizes the ugliness of ethnic conflict rather than Catholics massacring Catholics; the U.S. wars in Central America are charged to the Cold War account instead of Christians in the United States abetting the killing of Nicaraguan, Salvadoran, and Guatemalan Christians by one another. That no one describes these events as a scandal to the gospel, a cruel inversion of the unity of the body of Christ, is among the most embarrassing charges against contemporary Christianity.

THE WAY AND THE WAY NOT TAKEN

That the idea of ecclesial solidarity strikes contemporary Christians and others as an idea both foreign and disturbing testifies to the effectiveness of the modern project to subordinate and domesticate Christianity. For the past five hundred years, political and economic leaders have worked to undermine Christian unity and fragment the Church in the interests of nationalism, capitalism, and individualism. At the same time, the now-fragmented parts of Christianity—its ideas and institutions, liturgy and laity—have been enlisted as legitimation and cultural cement in service to the radical political, economic, and cultural transformations of modernity. So effective have these processes been that most Christians are frightened by what should have been part of their ecclesial life all along; those large parts of the Christian story (in Scripture, theology, and church history) in which something like ecclesial solidarity has existed have been ignored, rewritten, or caricatured.

Scripture scholars in recent decades have reminded us that just as Israel was created by Yahweh to be a contrast society set apart to instruct and edify the other nations of the world, so did the followers of Jesus see themselves in relation to the rest of the world.

The disciples of Jesus, those called out from the nations, leave their old identities and allegiances behind by being baptized into the Way of Christ. The claims of the biological family are qualified by bonds to one's brothers and sisters in Christ; markers of status and hierarchy are set aside in a community in which "there does not exist among you Jew or Greek, slave or free, male or female. All of you are one in Christ Jesus" (Gal 3:28).

This new type of human community, made possible by the Spirit, creates "a chosen race, a royal priesthood, a holy nation, God's own people, that you may declare the wondrous deeds of him who called you out of darkness into his marvelous light" (1 Pet 2:9).

Over and above the picture of a shared purse described in Acts 2 and 4, the New Testament presumes and recommends a high degree of mutuality, intimacy, and bonding among members of the Church. Gerhard Lohfink offers a brief sampler, which he describes as "far from exhaustive," on the centrality of the reciprocal pronoun "one another" (*allelon*) as a marker for the quality of real-world love and mutuality demanded of believers:

> outdo one another in showing honor (Rom 12:10);
>
> live in harmony with one another (Rom 12:16);
>
> welcome one another (Rom 15:7);
>
> admonish one another (Rom 15:14);
>
> greet one another with a holy kiss (Rom 16:16);
>
> wait for one another (1 Cor 11:33);
>
> have the same care for one another (1 Cor 12:25);
>
> be servants of one another (Gal 5:13);
>
> bear one another's burdens (Gal 6:2);
>
> comfort one another (1 Thess 5:11):
>
> build up one another (1 Thess 5:11);
>
> be at peace with one another (1 Thess 5:13);
>
> do good to one another (1 Thess 5:15);
>
> bear with one another lovingly (Eph 4:2);
>
> be kind and compassionate with one another (Eph 4:32);
>
> be subject to one another (Eph 5:21);
>
> forgive one another (Col 3:13);
>
> confess your sins to one another (Jas 5:16);
>
> pray for one another (Jas 5:16);
>
> love one another from the heart (1 Pet 1:22);
>
> be hospitable to one another (1 Pet 4:9);
>
> meet one another with humility (1 Pet 5:5);

have fellowship with one another (1 John 1:7).[1]

Lohfink adds that the early church, consistent with Jesus' example in the gospels,

> never considered capitulating to naïve dreams of "all men becoming brothers" or of "millions being embraced." In a very realistic manner they sought to achieve fraternal love within their own ranks and constantly made simultaneous efforts to transcend their boundaries. In this fashion an ever increasing number of people was drawn into the fraternity of the church, and new neighborly relations became possible.[2]

The earliest Christians would have found nothing exceptional in the idea of ecclesial solidarity. Early Christians saw themselves, and were seen by others, as more than just a new "religious" group, more than a new idea unleashed in the ancient world, and more than a voluntary club like other social groupings or associations.

As noted by Denise Kimber Buell in an important book, early Christians were more often seen as part of a new ethnic group, even a new race of people, in the Roman world. The focus of their worship was so distinctive, their way of life and priorities were so particular, that they were more properly seen as a *genos*, "a term widely used for Greeks, Egyptians, Romans and *Ioudaioi* [Jews]—groups often interpreted as ethnic groups or their ancient equivalents."[3]

Surveying a number of early Christian texts and narratives, as well as the literature of anti-Christian polemicists, Buell explains why early Christians referred to themselves as a distinct ethnic group or people in the world.

> First, race/ethnicity was often deemed to be produced and indicated by religious practices . . . Early Christians adopted existing understandings of what ethnicity and race are and how they relate to religiosity by reinterpreting the language of peoplehood readily available to them in the biblical texts they shared with . . . Jews, as well as political and civic language used broadly to speak about citizenship and peoplehood in the Roman Empire.[4]

1. Lohfink, *Jesus and Community*, 99–100.
2. Ibid., 114–15.
3. Buell, *Why This New Race*, 2.
4. Ibid., 2–3.

Second, she notes that although ethnicity and race were often used to indicated a fixity of identity, early Christians and their contemporaries also saw them as fluid and changeable categories. Further, that the concept of ethnicity/race was both fixed and fluid meant that Christians could make universal claims for themselves. "By conceptualizing race as both mutable and 'real,' early Christians could define Christianness both as a distinct category in contrast to other peoples (including Jews, Greeks, Romans, Egyptians, etc.) and also as inclusive, since it is a category formed out of individuals from a range of different races."[5]

The idea that one could "change" one's race or ethnicity seems impossible in a culture in which these are the quintessential ascriptive identities, largely unchangeable or immutable; for us, on the other hand, "religion" is a voluntary, changeable, and fluid part of identity, since one can "change" religions. But for Christianity in the early centuries, becoming part of the Christian "race" or ethnic community was available to all regardless of their communities or identities of origin—"conversion" was the process of changing races, of joining the peoplehood of Christ. In turn, the radical notion of conversion returns to the fore: it is best seen not as "a private matter of individual conscience resulting in an individual's affiliation with a religious movement, but explicitly as becoming a member of a people, with collective and public consequences."[6] And as she notes, "saying that Christianity was open to all was not mutually exclusive with defining Christians as members of an ethnic or racial group. In many early Christian texts, defining Christians as members of a people reinforces rather than conflicts with assertions of Christian universalism."[7]

Seeing oneself as part of a new race or ethnic group had undeniable political implications in the Roman world:

> [T]he spread of Rome's power blurred the lines of civic identity and ethnoracial identity, and religious practices helped to mark and redefine both citizenship and ethnic belonging. Christians likewise capitalized on this blurriness, refracting imperial discourse by avowing their citizenship in a different city (heavenly Jerusalem), under a different ruler, and by construing themselves

5. Ibid., 3.
6. Ibid., 46
7. Ibid., 138

as a people. In both civic and ethnic self-conceptions, religious practices serve as a primary vehicle for performing membership.[8]

[I]t is not sufficient to state that Christians formed a "religion" in contrast to a "race" or "ethnicity." Many early Christians described the consequence of belief in Christ (even though the kinds of belief varied widely) as acquiring membership in a people. When various believers in and followers of Christ (however understood) used ethnic reasoning, they were continuing a longstanding practice of viewing religious practices and beliefs as intertwined with collective identifications that overlap with our modern concepts of race and ethnicity, as well as nationality and civic identity.[9]

Historian Joyce Salisbury, among others, observes that Roman citizens took notice of the distinctiveness of their Christian neighbors, usually with disapproval.

Christians were perceived by their pagan neighbors to be antisocial in the deepest meaning of the word. They were creating their own society within the Roman one, and their loyalties were to each other rather than to the family structures that formed the backbone of conservative Roman society. Their faith led them to renounce parents, children, and spouses, and Romans believed this actively undermined the fabric of society. In fact, it did.[10]

While terms "race" and ethnicity mean very different things today, Buell's research reminds us that for Christians to think of themselves as joined first and foremost to one another, and only secondarily or derivatively to other corporate claimants on their affections and allegiances, is not a radical novelty in the Christian experience. Ecclesial solidarity in many respects is simply a more contemporary term for the same assumptions and aspirations—highlighting the sense in which God creates a new people from all existing nations and races, and the degree to which the worship of God and the practice of discipleship requires and keeps this people distinct and bonded to one another. Talk of the Church as its own "polis" or as a "community" in its own right may actually understate the extent to which conversion to Christ made for a new people in a strong sense of the term.

8. Ibid., 153
9. Ibid., 166
10. Salisbury, *Blood of the Martyrs*, 16.

Using "ecclesial solidarity" as its point of reference, this book explores a variety of issues and controversies facing contemporary Christianity in an era of globalization. One of the paradoxes of globalization is that while it constructs new transnational identities and communities, it also stimulates movements that reassert (and redefine) identities and allegiances in opposition to the effects of globalization: resurgent forms of nationalism, intensified ethnic/tribal identities, and separatist movements of various sorts. Some of these are longstanding issues with new wrinkles or implications, others are new issues that present the Church with novel temptations and opportunities.

The abandonment of the Church as a distinct race, a people drawn out and set apart by baptism, is a story told with various accents, agents, and agendas. For some, the co-optation of Christianity into the Roman Empire marks a decisive dilution of the Church as a community capable of creating and ordering affections, loyalties, and identities.[11] Others draw attention to the fragmentation of transnational Christianity at the hands of entrepreneurial state-builders in the early modern period, and the subsequent subordination of the churches (now plural, now competitive) to nationalism and its regimes.[12] Still others point to the role of Christian leaders and thinkers in facilitating these erosions of ecclesial coherence in the name of divine providence (e.g., Eusebius' "Oration in Commemoration of the Thirtieth Anniversary of Constantine"), theological and intellectual humility,[13] church reform and/or the progress and emancipations of the Enlightenment.

However the story is told, the ending is the same. The bonds of baptism are spiritualized and sidelined in favor of the blood-and-iron ties of patriotism and ethnonational solidarity, the dollars-and-cents sinews of capitalism, and the idolatry of modern and postmodern selves. In such a world it is unremarkable that Christian Hutus can slaughter Christian Tutsis the week after Easter; that Christian interrogators can torture Christian prisoners with impunity; that a Catholic military chaplain can bless the atomic bomb that destroyed the largest concentration of Catholics in Japan, including seven orders of nuns.

---

11. E.g., Kreider, *Violence and Mission*; Yoder, *Priestly Kingdom*.

12. E.g., Cavanaugh, *Myth of Religious Violence*.

13. See the argument of Milbank, *Theology and Social Theory*.

My argument is that the revitalization and reform of Christianity now and in the future will be both incomplete and doomed to irrelevance until it reclaims the integrity and distinctiveness of the Church. Unless the borders of baptism become capable of defining a people that "seek first the Kingdom of God," that sees itself as God's imperfect prototype for reconciled human unity in diversity (with the Sermon on the Mount as its "Magna Carta," in the words of Pope John Paul II), Christianity will continue its rapid descent into a parody of its calling and vocation.

Present and Prospective Realities

Charting the current dispositions of the churches in regard to ecclesial solidarity is a difficult matter, given the hetereogeneity of ecclesial life and thought; the gaps between theory and practice; and the overdetermination of nationalism on nearly all Christian traditions regardless of confessional theology or ecclesiology. At the risk of overgeneralization and caricature, the following sketch of Christianity in the United States may provide a sense of the contemporary situation:

- Roman Catholic and Orthodox ecclesiology see local congregations and the universal, transnational Church as mutually constitutive and essential for one another. In practice, the Orthodox concept of *symphonia* (partnership between national Orthodox churches and nation-states), and the de facto division of Catholicism into national churches, sharply constrain the transnational qualities of each.

- Mainline Protestantism, largely congregational in emphasis and national in scope (Anglicanism being a hybrid of Protestant and Catholic sensibilities), has not developed structures of ecclesiology in which the local and universal are essential to one another. The transnational nature of the Church is secondary and derivative in mainline practice, despite the increased importance accorded to ecumenical unity during the twentieth century.

- Evangelicalism ranges so broadly in its ecclesiology as to nearly defy description. The status of the Church ranges from inessential to a support group for the like-minded—radically congregational while sometimes part of a network of churches built by pastoral entrepreneurs. While this assortment of traditions remains staunchly nationalist in disposition, some distancing from nationalism has appeared due to ties with non-Western churches and disillusionment in some circles with the perceived secularism and anti-religious quality of Western culture.

- The Anabaptist movement remains strongly congregational in emphasis, but with substantive ties to other Anabaptist churches across national and political boundaries. Whereas Anabaptists historically have resisted institutions and practices designed to assimilate them into nationalist identities and allegiances, some contemporary Anabaptists pursue peace and justice goals in ways that move them closer to the theological and political dispositions typical of the bulk of American evangelicalism.

As even this simplistic overview suggests, the fashioning of a serious sense of baptism and ecclesial solidarity confronts obstacles in every branch of Christianity in the West. In that sense, no existing tradition can feel satisfied that it has settled on an optimal set of practices and commitments, nor is there an existing template to be copied from one part of Christianity to the rest.

And yet, the contemporary era presents new opportunities—theological, pastoral, and political-economic—for churches to develop a powerful sense of ecclesial identity and solidarity within and among themselves. The following sketch might suggest some of the dynamics and developments conducive to a greater expression of ecclesial solidarity in our time.

1) The increased salience of transnational consciousness and solidarity in other contexts affects popular assessments of what may be possible in an ecclesial context. If Amnesty International can build a worldwide community whose calling is human rights, if Greenpeace can inspire cadres worldwide to defy their own governments on a regular basis, and if the upsurge in global migration can begin complicating the claims of host-state nationalism, then people may stop seeing Christian solidarity as a far-fetched concept. One of the biggest obstacles to developing a stronger sense of ecclesial solidarity is the sense of hopelessness that surfaces whenever one contemplates challenging the demon-gods of nationalism and capitalism; yet, when people are encouraged to reflect on the ways in which their lives and loyalties are already impacted by transnational

claims and claimants, church-based initiatives may eventually seem less utopian and more within the realm of the possible.

2) The capacity of nations and states to demand loyalty from their subjects, at least in modern times, has rested on promises of personal security and economic adequacy. States are less able to deliver the goods in either respect in a world of globalizing markets, mobile capital, and violence and destruction from state and nonstate actors. The very notion of sovereignty is changing, as noted by theorists in international relations and international law—control of space gets one less than ever before, as mobility and fluidity increasingly trump the traditional powers of states. Perhaps the Church can embrace and claim a new sort of sovereignty for itself, a sovereignty without territory, identity without the sword. How ironic it may be that one of the oldest transnational communities—the Christian Church—may be among the first to negotiate a new and creative form of sovereignty as the stranglehold of the Westphalian system starts to weaken. If churches begin to find their security in God—as conveyed by their brothers and sisters in Christ—instead of from greater or lesser emperors and state benefactors, then the weakenesses of the state system may rebound to the benefit of the Church.

3) The powerful tools of various transnationalizing forces—revolutions in communications, reduced costs of transportation and travel, large groups of people at home in more than one place and culture—are at the disposal of the Church in its work of the Kingdom. In his new book, *Boundless Faith: The Global Outreach of American Churches*, sociologist Robert Wuthnow highlights an array of connections, practices, and relationships that enable and demonstrate the increased transnationalism of churches in the United States. His work focuses both on the sociological connections that might enable a rise in transnational identity and ethos in the future, as well as measures of such in the present,[14] and is worth exploring at length.

THE WUTHNOW ARGUMENT

Wuthnow claims that the internationalization of communications and travel are key factors driving the transnationalism of churches in the United States. He notes the quadroupling of international calls between 1991

14. See also Wuthnow and Offutt, "Transnational Religious Connections," 214

and 2004; the increase in air passengers going abroad (from 10 million to 60 million in 2000); and the fact that "nearly two-thirds (62 percent) of active church members in the United States have traveled or lived in another country. One in seven (14 percent) has lived in another country for at least a year."[15]

Further, he notes that some 42,000 American citizens are working abroad as full-time missionaries, 350,000 have spent between two weeks and a year as short-term mission volunteers last year, and likely more than one million have served for less than two weeks[16]; by his estimate, one-third of all congregations sponsored a mission trip in the past year, something on the order of 100,000 separate congregations.[17] Drawing upon several studies, he estimates that 1.6 million people per year are involved in short-term mission trips from the United States, and that between 20 and 25 percent of all church members could be involved in some sort of short-term mission trip in the course of their lifetime.[18]

In addition to those who actually travel abroad, millions of other American Christians participate indirectly in such efforts. Between 700,000 and one million churchgoers in the United States serve on mission committees, and as many as 16 million (out of 80 million active church members in total) "do volunteer work that they perceive to be of international benefit. In addition, at least 30 million members hear missionaries or international speakers, and 60 million give to international relief and hunger projects."[19] Seventy-four percent of U.S. church members report their congregation supported a missionary in the past year, while 48 percent reported their church hosted a guest speaker from another country during the same period

Wuthnow cites research indicating that 29 percent of church members in the United States report their congregations helped support a refugee or refugee family in the past year, a practice more frequent among Catholics and mainline Protestants (35 and 31 percent) than among evangelicals and black Protestants (25 and 22 percent).[20] Other scholars, most

---

15. Wuthnow, *Boundless Faith*, 3.
16. Ibid., 23.
17. Ibid., 168.
18. Ibid., 170–71.
19. Ibid., 175.
20. Ibid., 145–46.

notably Peggy Levitt, describe the significant effects and connections caused by large numbers of immigrant church communities and ethno-religious diasporas; countries of origin and of reception are both changed and brought closer together in a variety of ways.[21]

Wuthnow notes the considerable barriers to an increased sense of global connectedness among Christians posed by the profound local-ism of American ecclesial and secular culture. The typical congregation spends less than five percent of its revenue on a trans-local entity of any sort—from a denominational office to international church work:[22] he cites other scholars' work in suggesting that most congregational linkages are to other local congregations rather than to national or international bodies.[23]

Wuthnow does not discuss matters of nationalist socialization and church-based patriotism in describing the localist bias among American congregations. He does, however, take note of some by-products of Chris-tianity lived in the global dynamics of capitalism that reinforce the pri-macy of local identity. To him,

> the entrepreneurial ethos from the business world that infuses American culture . . . increasingly encourages a managerial style among clergy and other church leaders. The managerial style em-phasizes numeric growth as the premier sign of congregational success. It links clergy salaries, promotions, and prestige with at-taining this kind of success. It elevates congregational autonomy as a facilitator of such success, while identifying larger denomi-national structures as impediments. With potential congregants characterized by fewer denominational loyalties and greater ten-dencies to engage in denominational switching, the autonomous congregation that focuses on its own programs and local priori-ties is thus in the best position to succeed.[24]

> A related factor is the widely noted tendency for churchgoers to adopt the same consumerist mentality that they do in negotiating commercial transactions. The watchwords for this consumerist mentality are personal gratification and efficiency. Gratification means focusing first and foremost on satisfying one's personal

21. See Levitt, *God Needs No Passport*.
22. Wuthnow, *Boundless Faith*, 14.
23. Ibid., 14–15.
24. Ibid., 15.

needs and desires, including those of one's immediate family. Efficiency means doing so by incurring the least possible cost. Faced with making a decision among the various churches available in one's community, the religious consumer will thus choose the one that offers the best Sunday school program for one's children, the greatest chances of finding a suitable mate if one is single, the most convenient location, the most inspiring sermons, the clearest moral guidelines, or some other attractive feature, while avoiding such costs as having to spend money on programs from which there is no immediate personal benefit. Of course the calculations are never quite this crass or explicit. On balance, they nevertheless favor congregations that supply the most attractive incentives, secure the greatest commitment from their members, and keep the resulting resources in-house for the congregation's own growth and development.[25]

God's cosmic sense of humor may yet be revealed if the tools and effects of American-style globalization help to construct a sort of ecclesial solidarity capable of healing the most awful wounds of the body of Christ. Christians in the United States received a very early taste of this during the Central American wars of the 1980s as the United States sponsored a series of wars in El Salvador, Nicaragua, Guatemala, and Honduras. In a time before the internet, the official stranglehold on information was undermined by church workers in rural areas (where U.S.-supported slaughters were most plentiful) able to convey reports to their coreligioninsts in the U.S.; the reduced costs of travel made it possible for thousands of U.S. clergy and lay leaders to travel to and receive the hospitality of churches under siege, seeing for themselves the consequences of policies that previously would have benefited from the cloak of distance and obscurity; and church-owned media functioned to open new channels of daylight capable on occasion of piercing the propagandistic reporting orchestrated by the U.S. embassies and American reporters. Since then, the communicative instruments have multiplied and become more powerful even as their costs have fallen—the instrumentalities of building ecclesial solidarity are more abundant, and increasingly within reach financially of an ever-growing number of congregations and church bodies.

And they are beginning to have some measureable effects, according to Wuthnow. Despite the dominant localism of U.S. Christianity,

25. Ibid., 15–16.

church members overwhelmingly believe that solidarity with Christians abroad should be an important priority of churches in the United States. Five church members in six (84 percent) think their own congregations should emphasize "the work of Christians and Christian organizations in other countries," with 45 percent saying a lot of emphasis should be placed on this work. Only 4 percent say this work should receive no emphasis at all in their congregation. Evangelical Protestants are particularly likely to stress the importance of being connected with Christians abroad: 56 percent say their congregation should emphasize the work of Christians and Christian organizations in other countries a lot (37, 43, and 36 percent of mainline Protestants, black Protestants, and Catholics, respectively, give the same response).[26]

He notes that between 25 and 30 percent of congregations are involved in the issue of religious freedom in other countries, with pastors drawn into the concern due to a sense of solidarity.

This is the idea that Christians everywhere are part of the same body and thus should stand together with those who are being persecuted. In fact, pastors usually respond to broader questions of religious freedom and human rights by focusing on instances where Christians are being persecuted. In so doing, they often mention activities such as prayer vigils and awareness days that grew out of concerns about persecution in communist countries during the Cold War era.[27]

The overall effect, he argues, is that

As the world becomes increasingly interdependent, Christianity in the United States is becoming transcultural, responding to the realities of globalization by actively and intentionally engaging in activities that span borders. Transcultural congregations give priority to programs that honor their commitments at home but also seek to be engaged in the lives of others around the world. A transcultural orientation connects local commitments with churches, communities, organizations, and individuals in other countries. Church leaders increasingly stress having a vision that transcends the interests of those who gather for worship each week at the local church building. They contend that a congregation that focuses only on itself becomes insular. They want their

26. Ibid., 151.
27. Ibid., 158–60.

members to understand that the Christian gospel is for all humanity, and that they encourage members to become informed about and engaged with the full range of conditions to which Christian teachings apply. . . . [28]

Wuthnow's understanding of transnational ties and congregational life is not beyond criticism. He assumes no fundamental disconnect in theory or practice between Christianity and the operations of U.S. power in the world; he strives mightily to minimize the significance of American imperialism.[29] He argues that churches can and should work through the channels of mainstream politics on a variety of issues, without entertaining the possibility that such forms of participation might reinforce the sort of religious nationalism and bounded ecclesiology that he hopes to see leavened by a greater sense of transnational religious awareness.[30] His hopes that megachurches will be important forces for Christian transnationalism, given their resources and outreach internationally,[31] seems not to engage the nationalism typical of most of the largest megachurch ministries in the United States.

Still, what Wuthnow does is suggest that a call for exploring the nature and dynamics of what I call ecclesial solidarity is not a worthless exercise, one with no grounding in material practices, conditions, and opportunities. Unlike Wuthnow, however, I am less optimistic that sociological patterns by themselves will shape ecclesiological practices, beliefs, and loyalties. For those to change, a more robust notion of church must deepen and spread across congregations and movements. Such is neither automatic nor easy, but it is essential.

ECCLESIAL SOLIDARITY AND CHRISTIAN SOCIAL ETHICS

Needless to say, ecclesial solidarity sits athwart the assumptions underlying most approaches to Christian social ethics. While the Catholic Church calls for "solidarity" (by which it means wealthy countries and states being concerned for the welfare of poor ones), and uses the language of "communion" to highlight the unity of the Church worldwide (e.g., "Ecclesia in

28. Ibid., 6.
29. Ibid., 54.
30. Ibid., 188.
31. Ibid., 240.

America," to be discussed in a later chapter), its leaders assume all of this rests easily with strong notions of national citizenship and obligation to the state.[32] Orthodox Christianity draws the ties of baptism and nationalism tighter still, while Protestantism of several sorts largely privileges a sensibility of church-state partnership, often with a Reformed flavor.

Whether one sees civil authority as a product of the Fall (Augustine) or as a natural good in itself (Aquinas), ecclesial solidarity identifies a neglected aspect of ecclesiology and social ethics. It rejects the Niebuhrian choice of "responsible citizenship" as defined by the state, or passive withdrawal from the world's problems and needs. That Christians "benefit" in some way from the order constructed by political power does not make that order the "responsibility" of Christians—although state apologists since Roman times have attempted to make that argument. Origen's second-century rejoinder to Celsus stands as valid today: just by being what God wants it to be, the Church contributes to the world around it; and it need not serve the empire on the empire's terms in order to act "responsibly."

Similarly, the famous description of Christians as "resident aliens" in the *Letter to Diognetus* deserves extended reflection as one example of how the Church in one time and place saw itself as a unified body living among persons sharing other allegiances and gods:

> For the Christians are distinguished from other men neither by country, nor language, nor the customs which they observe. For they neither inhabit cities of their own, nor employ a peculiar form of speech, nor lead a life which is marked out by any singularity. The course of conduct which they follow has not been devised by any speculation or deliberation of inquisitive men; nor do they, like some, proclaim themselves the advocates of any merely human doctrines. But, inhabiting Greek as well as barbarian cities, according as the lot of each of them has determined, and following the customs of the natives in respect to clothing, food, and the rest of their ordinary conduct, they display to us their wonderful and confessedly striking method of life. They dwell in their own countries, but simply as sojourners. As citizens, they share in all things with others, and yet endure all things as if foreigners. Every foreign land is to them as their native country, and every land of their birth as a land of strangers. They marry, as do all [others];

32. See Catholic News Service, "To be a good Christian"; Global Zenit News, "Benedict XVI."

they beget children; but they do not destroy their offspring. They have a common table, but not a common bed. They are in the flesh, but they do not live after the flesh. They pass their days on earth, but they are citizens of heaven. They obey the prescribed laws, and at the same time surpass the laws by their lives. They love all men, and are persecuted by all. They are unknown and condemned; they are put to death, and restored to life. They are poor, yet make many rich; they are in lack of all things, and yet abound in all; they are dishonoured, and yet in their very dishonour are glorified. They are evil spoken of, and yet are justified; they are reviled, and bless; they are insulted, and repay the insult with honour; they do good, yet are punished as evil-doers. When punished, they rejoice as if quickened into life; they are assailed by the Jews as foreigners, and are persecuted by the Greeks; yet those who hate them are unable to assign any reason for their hatred.[33]

ECCLESIAL SOLIDARITY AND THE ISLAMIC "UMMA"

While the suggestion is likely to be a scandalous one to both parties, in some respects ecclesial solidarity resembles in some ways the Islamic notion of the "umma" as the primary allegiance and loyalty of Muslims worldwide. The transnational body of believers is meant to constitute one's most important identity, the needs of which take precedence over those of secular and national authorities on matters of highest importance.

While Islamic practice of transnational solidarity lags behind the utopianism of its vision, Garbi Schmidt notes the growing appeal of belonging to the global family of Muslims to younger Muslims worldwide and especially those living in secular and Western cultures. While appreciating the longtime international connections within the Islamic diaspora (usually bonding immigrants with their respective countries of origin), young people express increased dissatisfaction with the model of the "ethnic mosque" and the divisions of Muslims by country of origin and incorporation (or lack thereof) in one's home or host country.[34]

As Schmidt notes,

33. *Letter to Diognetus*, chap. 5.
34. Schmidt, "Transnational Umma," 576.

Among my own informants—young Muslim activists in the United States, Sweden and Denmark—a non-cultural, pristine interpretation of Islam is argued independent of regional or any other boundaries. Many argue that ethnic and national preferences and habits stand inferior to Islamic perceptions of identity and community, and they present themselves as Muslims before anything else. They share core values and practices as embedded in a well-scrutinized, genuine and "*ummatic*" vision of Islam.[35]

Schmidt notes further the importance of verse 49:13 in the Qur'an in this sensibility: "We created you as nations and tribes so that you may know each other." A verse like this, according to Schmidt's informants,

stresses not only aspects of equality, but asserts that nationality and ethnicity are irrelevant to a correct Islamic self-perception and practice. Islam as a creed includes everyone, and it calls for solidarity between believers in all parts of the world.[36]

Young Muslims, according to Schmidt, take advantage of electronic resources, use English as a transnational language, and seek out and share information on religious authorities and resources that affirm the transnational ties they seek to inhabit and deepen.

Similarly, Peter Mandaville notes that a transnational vision of Islamic solidarity acts as something of a "third space" that is neither integrated in immigrants' countries of origin or new residence.[37] Not all commentators see the deepening interest in the Umma as a sign of Islamic progress or increased global self-awareness: Olivier Roy, most notably, sees the move toward a "global Umma" as an act of desperation by Islamist activists who have met with repeated and widespread failures at the level of national politics.[38]

As will be seen in the chapters that follow, Christian ecclesial solidarity differs in many respects from at least some expressions of Islamic Umma as a source of loyalty and identity. What the two concepts share, among other things, is a recognition that their integrity as religious communities is threatened by the divisions created and sustained by secular actors like the modern state and global capitalism. No better illustration

35. Ibid., 577.
36. Ibid.
37. See Mandaville, *Transnational Muslim Politics*.
38. See Roy, *Globalized Islam*.

of this can be found than an article on "The Demands of Citizenship: Translating Political Liberalism into the Language of Islam." This wide-ranging piece by Andrew March explores whether the central doctrines of political liberalism can find support on explicitly Muslim terms within the tradition of Islamic political thought. The most crucial issue explored herein, however, seems to be how to derive a Muslim justification for Muslims to kill other Muslims at the behest of liberal states (via conscription, military service, etc.). While considering a variety of possible positions (depending on whether or not there is a draft, whether Muslims in the military might opt out of some activities based on religious objections to killing coreligionists), March concludes that ultimately the imperatives of liberalism must trump those of Islam: "A citizen cannot be affirming the legitimacy of his political community without, at the same time, recognizing its right to self-defence and survival. The bounds of reasonable pluralism cannot be stretched to the point of accepting other views."[39] Just as the transnational Church had to see its integrity and unity dissected to serve the ambitions of early modern state builders,[40] so too must Islam bow to the imperatives of liberal citizenship at the expense of transnational bonds among believers.

While I am persuaded that a strong expression of ecclesial solidarity most faithfully reflects the Church's call as a servant and herald of God's new people and kingdom, what that might mean in practice might admit of variations. Ecclesial solidarity requires communal discernment in the context of local churches formed to see themselves as part of the body of Christ, for whom borders and duties are less important than being part of the people called by God. One gathering of churches may conclude that it can participate selectively in worldly institutions of formative and ideological power—states and capitalist firms, for example—as long as they do not work against the needs of Christians (especially poor ones) elsewhere. In another context, Christians may see the need to define the differences between themselves and rival sources of identity and allegiance more starkly, counseling a conscientious non-participation (or a deligitimating

---

39. March, "Demands of Citizenship," 331.

40. See Cavanaugh, *Myth of Religious Violence*.

"participation without enthusiasm," in those areas where engagement is unavoidable) as a tactical matter vis-à-vis formative powers of allegiance and loyalty.

Lest one see in ecclesial solidarity an abandonment of the poor and oppressed, especially those who are not Christian, it bears noting that my proposal is an intermediate and not ultimate end. The hope is that a more unified Church will be better able to bring truly good news to the world's poor and oppressed of all sorts; the pathologies of a divided Church certainly have not helped the weakest (Christians and non-Christians) in the world, given the Church's inability to resist the siren song of war, the ravages of capitalism, and the selective compassion that privileges some (nations, races, trading partners) over others.

The chapters that follow do not "argue for" privileging ecclesial solidarity as much as attempt to illustrate how the world looks through the lenses of a strong sense of baptismal ties and of the body of Christ as one's defining allegiance. If these examples succeed in leading more Christians to loosen the presumed certainties of existing loyalties and affections, the community of discipleship might reposition or rank-order, reject or reaffirm, other types of allegiance and identity. The "borders of baptism," which reach beyond those of worldly time and space, might yet allow Christians to find their way amid the fragmented and partitioned map of the earthly city.

CHAPTER 2

Ad Intra:
Ecclesial Solidarity and World Christianity

A newcomer to the study of Christianity worldwide might be excused for thinking of Phillip Jenkins as the Christopher Columbus of the new "field" of world Christianity. For many people, this religious historian at Penn State University "discovered" a world just beyond the horizon of settled society in the affluent world, disclosing a vast and surprising geography waiting to be mapped, explored, and engaged. Beginning with the bestselling *The Next Christendom* and continuing through several later books and articles, Jenkins has done more than anyone to alert educated nonspecialists to the changes in Christianity's worldwide profile and composition.

Of course, like Columbus, Jenkins has "discovered" people who didn't know they were missing. For decades, scholars from various disciplines have noted the demographic shift within Christianity: with more than two-thirds of Christians living in Europe and North America in 1900, by 2000 roughly two-thirds resided in the "Southern" regions of the world (Africa, Latin America, and Asia). While church membership and participation levels have collapsed in much of Europe, population growth and conversions have increased Christianity's significance in relative and absolute terms in many poor countries and regions worldwide.

There in an undeniable faddishness attached to much of the contemporary enthusiasm for world Christianity. Journals and research centers, magazine features and sister-church programs, and media attention of all sorts—all of these are on the rise, and they contribute both to hope and hype about what it means to describe Christianity as a worldwide movement now based in the poorer sections of the world. There is no precedent for a so-called world religion like Christianity having changed its demographic profile so dramatically and in such a short period of time. Its implications for the future may be as immense as they are uncertain. Especially among Christians and scholars of Christianity in Europe and North America, world Christianity is now a major focus.

Much of this enthusiasm reflects projection of various sorts—church progressives see millions of Christians concerned about economic justice and human rights, while church conservatives cheer the prospect of new allies in the defense of orthodoxy and traditional sexual ethics. While many church leaders in the South appreciate their increased visibility and reinsertion into the narratives (and re-narration) of Christianity, some also note with concern the roles assigned to them in some more celebratory descriptions of "world Christianity." For all their growth and expansion, the churches in Africa, Latin America, and Asia are just as imperfect, just as challenged by sin and social problems, as are their wealthier cousins elsewhere

While hope for the cavalry riding over the hill (not to be confused with the hill of Calvary) explains part of the hype behind celebrations of the "world Christianity" paradigm, there is more at work than that. At least part of the enthusiasm for the new framework derives from what it replaces. By focusing on the active role of Christians in former colonial lands in creating and crafting their own churches and destiny, the centrality of Northern missionaries (and the guilt attendant to their ambiguous effects) will recede. What it means to be "church" and what difference it might mean to matters of politics and allegiance requires attending to the old framework as well as the one now taking shape.

CHRISTIANITY "WITHOUT THE EMPIRE"

The standard narrative is well known and needs only brief review. Christianity, the religion of Europe, hacked its way into Africa and Latin America, Asia and the Pacific, thanks to the sword's edge of colonial power and coercion. As noted by Dana Robert:

> [A]lthough missionary work often predated the coming of West-
> ern control, imperialism's arrival inevitably placed missions with-
> in an oppressive political context that they sometimes exploited
> for their own benefit. In China, for example, the unequal trea-
> ties of 1842 and 1858 permitted missions to operate in selected
> port cities and to buy land. Foreign missions in China benefited
> from extraterritoriality, whereby they were not subject to Chinese
> laws and regulations. In colonial Africa, missions received land
> grants. For example, in 1898 Cecil Rhodes awarded 13,000 acres
> to American Methodists for their Rhodesian mission . . . . While
> courageous individual missionaries mitigated the effects of im-
> perialism on indigenous peoples, by and large the missions ben-
> efited materially from European control. Most missionaries saw
> themselves as apolitical and preferred the status quo of colonial-
> ism to the uncertainties of nationalist revolution.[1]

The expectation of many observers—sympathizers and critics alike—
was that once the Europeans fell, so would their religion fade. For those
schooled by the mass media, developments of recent years seem to have
confirmed these assumptions—a rising Islam in some places, seculariza-
tion in others, and muscular capitalism in all places—and justified thinking that the Christianity of the colonies would go the way of all things.

In this respect, the "world Christianity" framework helps one see a
more complete and accurate picture, one now entering into congregational awareness in North America and Europe: that Christianity may be the
fastest-growing of the world religions, that its growth is overwhelmingly
in the former colonial regions of Africa, Latin America, and Asia, and
that the upsurge of faith in the Southern continents outstrips the considerable erosion of church membership and participation in the former
ecclesial centers of Europe and in parts of North America. Christianity is
once again a poor people's religion, and most of the churches of the North
are the old money in its midst—not as young or as strong as it used to be,
with hands firmly grasped on the patrimony and purse strings even as its
grip on the rudder of leadership weakens.

As the noted student of world Christianity, Andrew Walls, puts it:

> The last hundred years have seen the most considerable recession
> from the Christian faith to occur since the early expansion of Is-
> lam, and the area most affected has been Europe. A rather longer

1. Robert, "Shifting Southward," 50–51.

period has seen the most substantial accession to the Christian faith for at least a millennium, and that accession has taken place in the southern continents, especially in Africa, Latin America, and the Pacific. Always predicted by gloomy prophets, the pace of Christian recession has probably been faster than even the gloomiest expected. If the first open sign came when Holy Russia embraced an officially atheistic ideology, it eventually became clear that it bit most deeply within the open, liberal regimes of the West. And the accession of Christians in southern continents, so often regarded as the marginal effect of a misdirected missionary activity that largely failed, has been such as would have startled the most sanguine of the missionary fathers of 1792.[2]

Welcome to the semi-brave, semi-new world of "a post-Christian West and post-Western Christianity,"[3] an era in which Christianity must find its way "without the Emperor"—that is, without the favor, patronage, or benign neglect of nation-states, empires, or political authorities (I reserve the right to dissent from the notion that the "West" was previously and self-evidently Christian in any strong sense of the term). The sorts of alliances and working relations between the churches and secular powers typical of church-state relations in earlier times and places now literally seem inconceivable—the future of Christianity worldwide will depend on the church's own resources, skills, and practices rather than upon the benefices of rulers and protectors. While the formal apparatus of Christendom has long since disappeared, the West managed for several centuries with lower-grade forms of accommodation and détente, a variety of "neo-Constantinian" ideologies and exchanges of allegiance for assistance, legitimacy for protection.[4] Those days are dead in many places and dying in others; they do not represent the future of Christianity, despite the clinging desperation of many church leaders in the former core regions to prove their utility to state and economic powerholders.

Indeed, it is clear to me that one cannot explain the global resurgence of Christianity in terms of support from state institutions or their ministers. Rather than seeing the alliance of Christian missionaries with colonial powers as key forces in the worldwide growth of Christianity, Lamin Sanneh and others are more impressed by how the faith spread

2. Walls, *Cross-Cultural Process*, 31–32.

3. Ibid., 65.

4. See Yoder, *Priestly Kingdom*, esp. chap. 4.

once the "blessings" of colonial protection were removed. This explosion worldwide is overall more properly understood, in his view, by speaking of "the indigenous discovery of Christianity rather than the [Western colonial] Christian discovery of indigenous societies."[5] Having translated the Bible and the faith into indigenous languages and categories, the churches formed and inspired by missionaries—not to mention those many areas where Christianity predated colonialism, and including the countless numbers of autonomous Christian congregations outside missionary, denominational, or institutional control—did not collapse with the collapse of colonialism and missionary presence. On the contrary, as he notes, it is in this period—after 1945, after achieving national independence (oftentimes led by movements hostile to Christianity as a colonial import)—that the true explosion of Christianity arrives in many African countries. As he notes:

> Perhaps colonialism was an obstacle to the growth of Christianity, so that when colonialism ended it removed a stumbling block. A second factor was the delayed effect of Bible translation into African languages. With vernacular translation went cultural renewal, and that encouraged Africans to view Christianity in a favorable light. A third factor was African agency. Africans stepped forward to lead the expansion without the disadvantage of foreign compromise. Young people, especially women, were given a role in the church.[6]

Others note that the "blessings" of colonial alliance had long ago stopped paying dividends for the Christian churches. Indeed, the European churches found themselves working at odds with their putative state partners for much of the colonial period, as interests of state and commerce routinely thwarted missionary ambitions and priorities.

> By the end of the nineteenth century there is a clear note of embattlement in missionary literature, a sense of betrayal by the Christian state. At the beginning of that century, the great Islamic power had been the sultan of Turkey; by the end it was the British Empire, with the Royal Republic of the Netherlands in second place. The missionary interest was lamenting that Britain kept missionaries out of the emirates of northern Nigeria, that Britain was encouraging the Islamization of the Sudan. Furthermore, the

5. Sanneh, *Whose Religion?*, 10.

6. Ibid., 18.

British did these things more efficiently than the sultan ever did. In the twentieth century it appeared that the most considerable religious effects of imperial rule were the renovation and reformulation of a Hinduism that had seemed to be disintegrating at the time British rule was established, and a quite unprecedented spread of Islam. Colonial rule did more for Islam in Africa than all the jihads together.[7]

None of this should minimize the complicity of Christian mission enterprises with European colonialism, but the new world Christianity paradigm usefully returns agency to local Christians in colonized and postcolonial regions.

Transnational Christianity "after Christendom" is a remarkable movement, dizzying in its diversity and confounding in its complexity. And while the "politics of numbers" is a devilish affair—how to count the number of Christians given the range of standards for inclusion, problems of self-reporting, the immense fluidity of change and movement, and the occasional urge to inflate or deflate numbers for one reason or another—the rough estimates are adequate for present purposes. More than 60 percent of the world's Christians live in Africa, Asia, and the Pacific; both Africa and Latin America claim more Christians than does North America; the churches of Asia, Africa, and Latin America are all experiencing rapid growth levels, while North American Christianity shows only marginal growth and European churches are losing members.[8] The strongest communities of world Christianity seem to be Catholicism (1.1 billion adherents worldwide) and Pentecostal/Charismatic congregations (more than 570 million).

The future of world Christianity will likely be determined, in my view, by the interaction of Catholicism and Pentecostalism. Relations between the two largest branches of the Christian movement will shape the future of Christianity over the next century and longer; such relations will also figure significantly in whether and to what extent some sort of ecclesial solidarity will emerge during the same period of time.

Wilbert Shenk notes that

> Pentecostalism emerged at the beginning of the twentieth century as a socially nonconformed racially inclusive movement among

7. Walls, *Cross-Cultural Process*, 43–44.
8. Barrett and Johnson, "Annual Statistical Table."

the lower classes in the United States. Though the U.S. movement did not retain its racially inclusive stance for long, the Pentecostal/charismatic phenomenon today comprises a global community of some 534 million adherents. The movement has become a major force in world evangelization and has exerted deep influence on the global Christian community. . . .

The present strength of Pentecostalism arises in large measure from the fact that it has become indigenous throughout the world to an extent unmatched by other Christian traditions.[9]

Pentecostal forms of worship and spirituality have arisen both as independent forces worldwide and as extensions of existing Pentecostal communities (e.g., from the Azuza Street Revival, the mission work of the Assemblies of God). In its many variations and inculturations, Shenk notes that "the starting point is not rational discourse about the person and work of the Spirit but direct personal encounter with the Holy Spirit and the release of the charismata of the Spirit in the life of the believers."[10]

Pentecostalism is the young, vibrant, oftentimes combative expression of Christianity on the world stage. Some Pentecostal churches are openly disdainful of other Christian churches, others preach versions of the "health and wealth" gospel, while others still eschew concern for justice in favor of a fondness for authoritarian political regimes and movements. But the sheer size and reach of Pentecostalism ought caution one against excessive generalization, especially those that ascribe an inflexible insularity or ideological cast to churches of Pentecostal expression. Indeed, Pentecostalism is shaping and being shaped by its interactions with other Christian traditions and communions, oftentimes in ways relevant to future development of ecclesial solidarity. In Latin America, notes Leonildo Silveira Compos, one can see "Pentecostalized Protestantism" as well as "Protestantized Pentecostalism"; Catholics are learning from Pentecostals lessons about "personal caring, the sense of personal worth, the spontaneous manifestations of joy in worship, and the missionary outreach that empowers Pentecostal believers to share their faith openly."[11] Ralph Del Colle notes the emergence of Pentecostal-Roman Catholic dialogues at many levels, exploring matters of sanctification and finding common ground in their understanding of "conversion as the framework

9. Shenk, "Recasting Theology of Mission," 100–101.

10. Ibid., 102.

11. See George, "Brazil."

for a theology of grace" and "the affective dimension of human experience as a resource for theological anthropology."[12]

> In their turn, Pentecostals are learning both from non-Pentecostal Protestants and from Catholics to value formal theological education and to develop a more systematic theology. Dialogue with Pentecostals has resulted in more authentic contextualization in worship for Protestants and Catholics, and Pentecostals have emulated Catholic base ecclesial communities.[13]

Other scholars note the capacity within Pentecostalism both for ecumenical unity and ecclesial independence, cross-national ties and perhaps ecclesial solidarity.[14] Others caution against using the term "Pentecostal" as a blanket term, especially one with negative connotations (a special temptation of Northern Christians, for whom the label of "fundamentalist" comes too easily off the tongue).[15] Even the associations of Pentecostalism with right-wing politics are increasingly unhelpful, given the rise of significant movements for ecology and economic justice within at least some Pentecostal fellowships.[16]

WORLD CHRISTIANITY AND ECCLESIAL SOLIDARITY

Ecclesial solidarity, or a sense of the transnational ties and unity of the church, remains an underdeveloped theme in much of the scholarly and popular writing on world Christianity. Still, several of the founding voices in the field recognize the importance of such an ecclesial vision, and identify some trends testifying to its viability in various local congregations and contexts.

As noted in chapter 1, ecclesial solidarity is not a straightjacketed homogenization of faith, nor an imposition of power that denies the integrity of the local church. On the contrary, the absence of ecclesial solidarity across national, ethnic, and other divides has allowed pathologies to fester within churches North and South; the integrity and mission of the churches require the local and universal to exist in a dialectical interplay

12. Del Colle, "Pursuit of Holiness."

13. George, "Brazil."

14. Jenkins, *Next Christendom*, 63–72.

15. Robert, "Brazil."

16. E.g., Shenk, "Recasting Theology of Mission."

of creativity and correction. Walls describes this as the necessary complementarity of the "indigenizing principle" (guaranteeing that Christianity will adapt and embrace the best of all cultures worldwide, allowing for the faith to be "at home" in each culture) and the "pilgrim principle" (which makes Christianity transformative of all cultures worldwide rather than be absorbed by them).

> The Christian has all the relationships in which he was brought up, and has them sanctified by Christ who is living in them. But he has also an entirely new set of relationships, with other members of the family of faith into which he has come, and whom he must accept, with all their group relations (and "disrelations") on them, just as God has accepted him with his. Every Christian has dual nationality, and has a loyalty to the faith family which links him to those in interest groups opposed to that to which he belongs by nature . . .
>
> In addition . . . the Christian is given an adoptive past. He is linked to the people of God in all generations (like him, members of the faith family), and most strangely of all, to the whole history of Israel, the curious continuity of the race of the faithful from Abraham. By this means, the history of Israel is part of Church history, and all Christians of whatever nationality, are landed by adoption with several millennia of someone else's history, with a whole set of ideas, concepts, and assumptions which do not necessarily square with the rest of their cultural inheritance; and the Church in every land, of whatever race and type of society, has this same adoptive past by which it needs to interpret the fundamentals of the faith. The adoption into Israel becomes a "universalizing" factor, bringing Christians of all cultures and ages together through a common inheritance, lest any of us make the Christian faith such a place to feel at home that no one else can live there; and bringing into everyone's society some sort of outside reference.[17]

In what I find to be a powerful and potent suggestion, Walls further notes that:

> It is not possible to have too much of the localizing and indigenizing principle which makes the faith thoroughly at home, nor too much of that universalizing principle which is in constant tension with it, and which links that local community with its "domestic"

17. Walls, *Missionary Movement in Christian History*, 9.

expression of faith in the same Christ of Christians of other times and places. It is possible only to have too little of either.[18]

The political significance of an adequate balance should not be obscured. As Shenk notes:

> Whenever the Christian Gospel truly encounters a culture it disturbs the status quo, altering the normal state of things that gives human beings identity. It exposes the fact that no culture is wholly submitted to the kingdom and rule of God. In every culture an array of principalities and powers contends for human allegiance. In the face of this reality the Gospel asserts that in Jesus the Messiah, God has acted decisively to liberate humankind from sin. In the Incarnation "the Logos became flesh" precisely to expose the false claims of these other powers and establish the means for men and women to be reconciled to God in Jesus Christ. Thus, the question at stake in every context is always that of allegiance: is Jesus Christ Lord? And wherever Jesus Christ is not acknowledged as Lord, the church is called to evangelize.[19]

The contemporary enthusiasm for contextualizing Christianity—making it an authentic part of local cultures rather than an alien imposition from beyond—in no way changes the need for a critical integration of universalizing and localizing tendencies. According to one of the most important voices for contextual Christianity, in a passage overlooked by many lesser champions of Christian diversity, one must not ignore the pitfalls of theologies

> in which "context" determines what we value and do not value in religion. Context is not passive but comes preloaded with its own biases, ready to contest whatever claims it encounters. Contexts, after all, are constructed strategies. As such, a context-sensitive approach should be responsive without being naïve.[20]

There will not, and should not be, a single "global Christian culture," uniform and unreflective of the legitimate gifts of diversity and variety that God has bestowed on the church. Rather, ecclesial solidarity will be a constellation of different Christian cultures—reflecting the particularity of their cultures of origin, drawing up into themselves the best of those

18. Ibid., 30.

19. Shenk, "Recasting Theology of Mission," 99.

20. Sanneh, *Whose Religion?*, 4–5.

cultures as they are redirected toward the worship of God and service to humanity. While in some cases collegiality among churches is facilitated by shared ecclesial structures, structures in themselves may guarantee nothing. Further, Christian congregations—even of very different origin and trajectory—have found themselves able to recognize and support one another in the absence of formal bonds, creedal statements, or linkages. This last point is important, lest one presume that a formal ecumenical structure (like the World Council of Churches) is a prerequisite for the cultivation and sustenance of ecclesial solidarity as I understand it. In discussing the early African churches that existed formally outside the Roman empire, Walls notes that they "recognized an organic link with Christians far away, brought about by their Christian allegiance. They saw themselves as part of a world community." From ancient times into the twenty-first century, those ties have remained. With African Christianity as an example, Walls notes that:

> The sense of an umbilical cord connecting Ethiopia with the outside world through the years of its isolation is a remarkable witness to Christian universality. That theme, that Christians in some way belong to one another across geographical, political, and ethnic frontiers, is bound to recur . . . .[21]

Jenkins notes that the churches of Latin America already recognize themselves as part of a common community of faith, while a similar consciousness is emerging in different ways among large portions of African Christianity. As of yet, however, the two continental communities of churches have only begun to interact with one another in a significant degree.

> The resulting segregation of interests and ideas is remarkable, since the churches in Africa and Latin America share so many common experiences . . . [A] period of mutual discovery is inevitable. When it begins—when, not if—the interaction should launch a revolutionary new era in world religion. Although many see the process of globalization as yet another form of American imperialism, it would be ironic if an early consequence was a growing sense of identity between Southern Christians.[22]

21. Walls, *Cross-Cultural Process*, 88–89.

22. Jenkins, *Next Christendom*, 12.

It would be presumptuous to assume that these processes of Christian recognition and affirmation will invariably be contained within the received Western categories of Protestant-Catholic-Orthodox. Dana Robert argues that "the forms and structures for the growth of late twentieth-century Christianity could not be contained within either the institutional or the theological frameworks of Western Christianity."[23] Once again, Walls puts the matter best:

> We have become used to the assumption that Christianity exists in three more or less permanent modes: Roman Catholic, Protestant, and Orthodox. These categories, however, reflect events in Western history; in the West they have a significance that they cannot have in the non-Western world. They will continue to be valid outside the West as indicators of organization and affiliation, but they will likely become less and less useful as descriptors. A large segment of African Christianity, for instance, cannot be called either Catholic or Protestant in any meaningful sense: it is simply African. Furthermore, its features are to be found among thousands of African believers whose affiliation is Catholic or Protestant. There are "traditions" in the Christian world community today that reflect modes of Christian existence in the same way as the labels "Catholic," "Protestant," and "Orthodox" have hitherto done. It seems likely that if we are to acquire historical understandings of Christianity as a non-Western religion, the reception of the categories by which Christians have been described will be required.[24]

How Ecclesial Solidarity Affects World Christianity: One Scenario

Ecclesial solidarity, in my view, is essential if the church is to witness faithfully to its commission to form a new people, a gathering of the nations, and to stand however imperfectly as a foretaste of the kingdom of God—in which the poor are fed, enemies are reconciled, and forgiveness rather than revenge rises up from sin and predation. It is also essential as something the world needs, whether or not the principalities and powers know it. Nationalism is a dead end, capitalist globalization is a carnival

23. Robert, "Shifting Southward."
24. Walls, "Eusebius Tries Again."

35

showman's shell game, and ethnic/identity politics ends with people talking only to themselves and carrying a knife beneath their cloak.

One of the regrettable consequences of the weakening of ecclesial integrity in the modern world allows for aspects of Christian theology and practice to be used by secular powers against the welfare of the Church and its mission. Elsewhere I have described how this plays out in the arena of culture industries—with Christian narratives, symbols, songs, and metaphors turned against believers by advertisers and marketers.[25] Another, more immediately dangerous, example of this concerns the hijacking of the just-war tradition.

Whatever else one might say about the more technical aspects of Augustine's thought, it seems clear to me that his understanding of just war presupposed a transnational church essentially unified and encompassed by an overarching political body that itself recognized the authority of the church. It would have been inconceivable to him that his just-war principles could be used to justify war of one Christian kingdom against another kingdom—or that the church had given over to worldly authority the ultimate determination of whether war was just *for the church*. Since for Augustine the Christian world was coterminous with the Roman Empire, it was not possible for the Empire's wars to be aimed at other Christian communities or polities (the question of force against heretics was justified in terms of mercy, not just war). And since the empire was a single political entity, its internal conflicts were not matters of legitimate kingdoms or authorities squaring off against one another as did states after the modern period.

And yet, consider the absurdities of our time. The dominance of states as institutions has given rise to warring parties all claiming the mantle of a just war for their cause—with church leaders aplenty blessing their efforts. All the combatants in World War I claimed to be fighting a just war—and the ecclesial establishments in each of them approved the scandal of Christians killing other Christians upon the orders of Christian or non- or semi-Christian rulers. Church leaders on all sides of the World War II ceded to their respective Caesars the legitimacy of just war, then stood by helplessly as the principles of "jus in bello" were eviscerated by extermination camps, mass firebombings, and the twin crimes of Hiroshima and Nagasaki.

25. See Budde, *(Magic) Kingdom of God*; Budde and Brimlow, *Christianity Incorporated*.

In our day, state leaders don't even wait for nationalist church leaders to pronounce on matters of just war. Just-war criteria are detached from the church, transformed into a checklist to be used by anyone—religious or not, malevolent or not—who seeks salve for conscience and passion from soldiers and the home front. George W. Bush didn't wait for church leaders to pronounce on whether his war on Afghanistan was a just war, nor did he consult with the church universal in the run-up to his attack on Iraq. Such would have struck him as beside the point—indeed, some Christian commentators suggested that, given the high quality of the "intelligence" available to him as leader of the most powerful nation on earth, he was better positioned to decide the justice of the war than lowly church leaders. In this view, church leaders should be followers, accepting the determinations of the leader and providing chaplaincy to a society in mobilization.

The ineffectual attempts of the Vatican to remind the world that the Church might have a say in whether a given war might be just illustrates the dilemma faced by a fragmented Christianity in which ecclesial solidarity is anemic. Pope John Paul II argued against the attack on Iraq for months, Vatican diplomats said the just-war criteria had not been met, and Catholic and Protestant leaders in the United States and around the world mostly opposed the war in advance. To no effect. Christian solders marched off obediently, unencumbered by ecclesial calls for noncooperation or resistance because such never came—having given over to Caesar the determination of what constitutes a just war, at least in the minds of the faithful, and having no effective links with churches elsewhere, church leaders reverted to embarrassed silence where they did not lapse back further into their familiar posture of "supporting the troops" no matter the cause or circumstances.

A developed sense of ecclesial solidarity might be one way for proponents of just-war theory to repair this major structural defect in the doctrine's theological integrity. Imagine the implications if, when a secular leader proclaims a "just war" in the offing, church leaders from around the world met to consider the claim. Imagine these church leaders engaging in a process of mutual discernment, involving ecclesial communities from those regions directly affected (the warring parties, for example) as well as from the larger Christian world. One could imagine a determination from such a body that a given conflict does or does not meet Christian criteria of a "just" war. If it does, the burden of hard choices—of judgment, as Oliver O'Donovan would say[26]—in a fallen world falls on the entire Christian community, for which reconciliation and repentance afterward are in order. If it does not, perhaps these assembled church leaders would suggest that no Christian could faithfully participate in such an unjust conflict, which would then fall into categories of homicide condemned by the Christian tradition. Those who follow the counsel of the churches instead of the dictates of state could then draw upon the hospitality, support, and prayers of brothers and sisters in Christ from around the world.

Of course, such a circumstance is fantasy so long as the sectarian categories of citizenship or peoplehood trump one's membership in the body of Christ. In this, the alleged collectivism of the Catholic tradition is as impotent as the aggregate of free agents gathered in most Protestant congregations—let the Pope say whatever the Pope wants, but Catholics will march off to kill other Catholics with impunity, even as many Protestants wait in vain for a voice to speak across the divides of denomination, class, and region. The dominance of nationalism over Christian universalism, described effectively by historian Adrian Hastings, continues apace despite the momentary shame felt by church leaders over ecclesial sanctioning of intra-Christian slaughters like World War I—a shame that itself was unable to resist the same sort of embrace during World War II.[27]

A developed ecclesial solidarity—which I have already described as the conviction that "being a Christian" is one's primary and formative loyalty, the one that contextualizes and defines the legitimacy of other claimants on allegiance and conscience—could help rid the world of the scandal of Christians killing other Christians in the name of a secularized Christian ethic wielded by secular authorities. And when Christians get to the point when they might be less willing to kill their brothers and sisters in Christ, they might also come to reconsider the killing of their non-Christian brothers and sisters, whom God also loves and for whom Jesus came to bring good news.

26. See O'Donovan, *Just War Revisited*.
27. Hastings, "Christianity and Nationhood," 257.

WORTH WATCHING? ORTHODOX CHRISTIANITY, SOLIDARITY, AND WORLD CHRISTIANITY

The world Christianity paradigm looks to be a fruitful one for scholars and congregational leaders alike. It seems likely to facilitate research and reflection across a wide range of issues related to Christian life and thought, multiplying foci and frameworks in important and useful ways. One area awaiting further exploration within a world Christianity framework also bears directly on the prospects for ecclesial solidarity—namely, the present and future of Orthodox Christianity.

To date, most English-language scholarship on world Christianity has focused on the global South or areas of Western (Latin) Christianity. The Orthodox churches have received less attention despite their multinational character and size; one anticipates greater attention to Orthodoxy as part of the evolution of the world Christianity framework.

At first blush, prospects for ecclesial solidarity seem distinctly unpromising when one considers the significance of the Orthodox traditions followed by a fifth of the world's Christians. With the unity of Byzantium shattered and replaced by a family of thirteen autocephalus (autonomous, usually nationally or ethnically based) Orthodox churches, congregational cooperation and bonds within Orthodox communities are no easy matters; further, many of the most powerful actors within Orthodoxy remain skeptical of efforts toward greater cooperation, much less visible unity, with Catholicism and Protestantism.

Victor Roudemetof notes that Orthodoxy embraced political nationalism in the nineteenth century, leading to what he calls

> the nationalization of Orthodoxy. By this term I mean the particularization of a formerly universalistic religion, whereby God becomes in effect not a universal God, but the God of a particular nation.[28]

> During globalization's contemporary period and perhaps more evidently after the collapse of communism in Eastern Europe, the national churches' re-territorialized religiosity favors the maintenance and strengthening of local institutions that allow the preservation of the church-nation link . . . Their goal is to assert their

---

28. Roudemetof, "Greek Orthodoxy," 71–72.

modern synthesis of church and nation in the face of contemporary globalization.[29]

In discussing the relations between the powerful Moscow Patriarchate and the rest of the Orthodox world, Alicja Curanovic notes that "although theoretically the Universal Orthodox Church should be unanimous, the decentralized structure of the Orthodox world means that the individual churches often have divergent interests. Just like states, the churches govern their canonical territories, compete and form alliances."[30]

Similarly, she notes that while the family of orthodox churches qualifies as a transnational religious subject, and that the several churches have much freedom due to egalitarianism and decentralization among them, such traits

> also bind them to their states more strongly than is the case with other religious organizations. The traditionally close relations between Orthodox churches and their state authorities have been determined by historical factors, including the concept of *symphonia*' that has applied to the Eastern Orthodox Church for centuries. What ties state and church together is the specific sphere of common interest. A consequence of the fact that churches and states act on the same territory is the fact that they share some interests, which motivates them to cooperate in both domestic and foreign policy. Another result of a symbiotic relation of this kind between the state and an Orthodox church is the phenomenon of the *internalization* of Orthodoxy, which manifests itself in the binding of religion with such phenomena as ethnicity, national myths, and patriotism.[31]

Yet even here, however, countervailing trends open space for greater ecclesial cooperation and transnational solidarity. Competition among Orthodox partriarchates (Moscow, Constantinople, Greece) has caused some Orthodox leaders to seek out alliances and deeper ecumenical ties with the Vatican and major Protestant communities; the Ecumemical Patriarchate in recent years has come to stress its transnational responsibilities, and has begun to convince believers that its decisions should take precedence for believers over the decisions of national governments.[32]

29. Ibid., 85–86.

30. Curanovic, "Attitude of the Moscow Patriarchate," 301.

31. Ibid., 302.

32. Roudemetof, "Greek Orthodoxy," 85.

As Curanovic notes,

> The two patriarchates (Moscow and Constantinople) . . . compete for the right to represent Orthodoxy worldwide. In order to achieve this goal both churches have to establish relations with non-Orthodox transnational subjects and exercise an active foreign policy. In the international arena, Constantinople tries to present itself as an open and progressive church, in contrast to a benighted and xenophobic Russian Orthodox Church. The contrast is clear in the attitudes of the patriarchates toward the Vatican. While Moscow keeps refusing to allow the pope to make an official visit to Russia and considers ecumenism a kind of "Catholic proselytism," Constantinople emphasizes the need for the cooperation of all Christians in order to stop the secularization of Europe. The warm welcome which Pope Benedict receive in Phanar in autumn 2006 had a significant and positive impact on the image of the ecumenical patriarch. The common prayer of the two hierarchs and their declaration of cooperation on behalf of Christian Europe were widely seen as a serious step toward rapprochement between the western and eastern churches. The fact that the Moscow Patriarchate is not participating in this initiative weakens its position in Europe.[33]

And where national Orthodox communions have seen their members killing one another as part of national military clashes among their governments,[34] national patriarchs have called for peace as a matter of ecclesial unity—no small matter especially given that the Russian patriarch, Aleksy II, is seen as a reliable ally of the Kremlin in almost all policy areas.

As noted by Sophia Kishkovsky, "The Russian conflict with Georgia is the first fighting between nations peopled by a majority of Orthodox Christians and not under Communist rule since the Second Balkan War in 1913 pitted Serbia, Greece, Montenegro and Romania against Bulgaria in a prelude to World War I." Aleksy II issued a statement on August 8, 2008, that lamented that "Orthodox Christians are among those who have raised their hands against each other. Orthodox peoples called by the Lord to live in fraternity and love are in conflict." Two days later, Kishkovsky notes, Patriarch Ilia II of Georgian Orthodox Church said in a sermon

---

33. Curanovic, "Attitude of the Moscow Patriarchate," 309.
34. Kishkovsky, "Conflict Test Ties."

that "one things concerns us very deeply—that Orthodox Russians are bombing Orthodox Georgians."[35]

At least one student of Orthodox politics, Adrian Pabst, draws attention to the drive by Moscow patriarch Kirill to gain greater independence from the Russian state while building transnational unity among Orthodox communions.

> By forging closer ties with other Orthodox churches, Kirill is determined to reassert the trans-national character of Orthodoxy. On his first visit as patriarch in Constantinople at the beginning of this month, he appealed to the common theological tradition that binds together the Orthodox sister churches. Crucially, he also described the ecumenical patriarch of Constantinople as the new Rome that safeguards the unity of all local communions across the Orthodox world.[36]

Pabst notes that Kirill's agenda looks less like the imperialistic subordination of church to state typical of the Moscow Patriarchate in the past, and instead "underscores his continued commitment to a shared supranational Orthodox identity." Combined with domestic successes of various sorts, he has initiated "potentially a stunning reversal of the widely perceived subordination of the Orthodox church to the Russian state," a crucial step in building real unity in the Orthodox world.

In other words, despite the nationalist character of much contemporary Orthodoxy, ecclesial solidarity of some sort is not beyond reach. As with cooperation of churches across borders elsewhere, it is likely to be episodic, driven by local needs and contingent events as much as by theological commitments. As paradigm and reality, world Christianity requires and makes room for ecclesial solidarity in ways likely to endure in the years ahead. As Orthodox communions find their way in the changing contexts of world Christianity and the global political economy, ecclesial solidarity may become more compelling and salient in ways not apparent in the past.

35. Ibid.
36. Pabst, "Kirill Is not the Kremlin's Man."

PART II

Examining the Hard Cases through an Ecclesial Lens

CHAPTER 3

Global Identity:
How Not to Proceed[1]

*Humankind no longer has the luxury of letting such a [global] ethic
slowly and haphazardly grow by itself, as if it willy-nilly will happen. It is
vital that there be a conscious focusing of energy on such a development.
Immediate action is necessary.*

—Leonard Swidler[2]

*Since no enduring civilization—indeed, no viable society within a
civilization—has developed without a dominant religion at its core, and
it is unlikely that a globalized civilization, or the structures of civil society
likely to populate it, can develop in creative ways without one either, it
makes a great deal of difference which religion becomes dominant, how it
does so, and how it treats other religions.*

—Max Stackhouse[3]

1. Earlier versions of some material in this chapter were presented as "The Global Context of Catholic Social Engagement," to the Institute of Pastoral Studies, Loyola University, September 15, 2006; and "Rational Faith in a Global World?" to The Grandeur of Reason: Religion, Traditionalism, and Universalism, a conference sponsored by the Center for Theology and Philosophy, Rome, Italy, September 1–4, 2008.

2. Swidler, "Toward a Universal Declaration," 341.

3. Stackhouse, "General Introduction," 52.

*America was created as a Protestant society just as and for some of the
same reasons Pakistan and Israel were created as Muslim and Jewish
societies in the twentieth century.*

—Samuel Huntington[4]

INTRODUCTION

In recent years, three major projects have sought to engage Christian
scholarly and pastoral energy in addressing the globalization of politics,
economics, culture, and religion. While they have much in common,
these ventures display significant differences in their objectives and approaches. In this chapter I offer a brief review and critique of these, with
an eye toward contributing to the discussion of reason and Christian discipleship in our so-called global era. The first of these projects is the "Declaration Toward a Global Ethic," drafted by Hans Küng and associated
with the 1993 Parliament of the World's Religions.[5] The second initiative
is the "God and Globalization" project, directed by Max Stackhouse and
supported by the Center of Theological Inquiry at Princeton Theological
Seminary. The third is the "Clash of Civilizations" discourse initiated by
and identified closely with the late Samuel Huntington, professor of political science at MIT.

In order for the notion of ecclesial solidarity to receive a fair hearing within Christian circles, certain more prominent ideas (like the three
mentioned above) must be assessed theologically and set aside. While
what follows is far from a comprehensive appraisal of globalization and
Christianity,[6] one hopes it demonstrates that no already existing position
offers an obviously superior understanding of how the churches ought
to understand identity and the global now and into the future. Clearing
the conceptual underbrush with reference to these three major schools of
thought seems like a modest but necessary step.

4. Huntington, *Clash of Civilizations*, 63.

5. Küng and Kuschel, *Global Ethic*. Further citiations will be given parenthetically in
the text.

6. For one attempt at a broader treatment, see Waalkes, *Fullness of Time*.

DECLARATION TOWARD A GLOBAL ETHIC

The 1993 Parliament of the World's Religions met in Chicago as both centennial celebration of the initial Parliament—held in 1893 in conjunction with the World's Fair hosted in that city—and as a new initiative in interfaith cooperation and activity. The 1993 group asked Professor Küng to provide the working draft of a statement on global ethics derived from consultation among major religious traditions and scholars. The finished product was eventually endorsed on behalf of the Parliament, and has been both a focal point of discussion and activity in its own right, and also a reference point for similar groups interested in global ethics (e.g., the project associated with Professor Leonard Swidler of Temple University, whose quote began this chapter).

Küng notes that he was well aware of the difficulties in crafting a declaration that addressed serious global problems while steering between substantive particularity—drawing only from Christian or Muslim categories, for example—and ethical minimalism of the least-common-denominator sort. The way forward, to him, could only be an inductive, phenomenological one—to discern "what is already common to the religions of the world now despite all their differences over human conduct, moral values and basic moral convictions. In other words, a global ethic does not reduce the religions to an ethical minimalism but represents the minimum of what the religions of the world already have in common now in the ethical sphere" (7–8).

What are these already existing ethical postures commonly held across the world's religions? According to Küng and the Parliament, there are four:

1. "Commitment to a culture of non-violence and respect for life"

2. "Commitment to a culture of solidarity and a just economic order"

3. "Commitment to a culture of tolerance and a life of truthfulness"

4. "Commitment to a culture of equal rights and partnership between men and women"

Even before one begins to look more deeply into these four common convictions, the Global Ethic gives evidence of slippage at the level of method. On the one hand, these general commitments are said to be "things which we already hold in common and which we jointly affirm, each on the basis of our own religious or ethical grounds" (22). On the other hand, there is an undeniable imperative of persuasion and indeterminacy about these assertions—the drafters felt compelled "to express what the fundamental elements of a global ethic *should be*" (21, emphasis added). Convincing people of how things should be would be unnecessary if the aforementioned principles were truly shared. This paradox—or contradiction, if one is less charitably inclined—runs through this and other similar projects in global ethics—considerable energy expended to tell people what they already believe that simultaneously tells them what they should believe. The reasoned inductivism of the method finds itself compromised repeatedly along the way.

Not surprisingly, the ethical underpinnings of the Global Ethic initiative is unapologetically Kantian. As the document states:

> There is a principle which is found and has persisted in many religious and ethical traditions of humankind for thousands of years: *What you do not want done to yourself, do not do to others!* Or in positive terms: *What you wish done to yourself, do to others!* This should be the irrevocable norm for all areas of life, for families and communities, for races, nations and religions. (24–25)

Or, in even shorter form, "our religious and ethical convictions demand that *every human being be treated humanely!*" Similarly, "every human is obliged to behave in a genuinely human fashion, to *do good and avoid evil!*" (23, emphasis in original).

The Global Ethic's approach to rationality—a universal reason devoid of history and place which yields (or is told it should yield) statements infused with several magnitudes of abstraction—is one that seeks to be its own justification. As my colleague at DePaul University, Professor Scott Paeth, notes, the invocation of the Golden Rule in the Global Ethic statement is grounds not only for the specifics that follow from it (equality before the law, freedom of speech and religion, and the like), but also for what precedes it (human rights, ecological concern, calls for justice and peace). With both its founding principles and so-called middle principles grounded in the Golden Rule, Paeth notes that "the Golden Rule is itself the presupposition of the presuppositions."[7]

Persons invested in the Global Ethic approach to reasoned discourse across religious traditions have different assumptions about the future

7. Paeth, "Shared Values," 410 n. 12.

status of existing religions in the globalizing future. For Küng, the Dec-laration spells out an "ethical minimalism" whereas the world's varied sacred scriptures offer a "maximal ethic." Over time, he hopes that the realm of shared ethical minimalism will expand and deepen (73). Further, the Declaration is intended to prompt reflection and change within exist-ing religious traditions (69)—again, a curious aspiration in a project that legitimates itself by being primarily a descriptive enterprise focused on already existing consensus.

Other advocates of a Kantian global ethic are more forthright in the transformative ends built into the approach to rationality they employ. Swidler, for example, suggests that the ethical traditions of existing re-ligious communities—Buddhists, Christians, Marxists—must be super-seded by the development of a global ethic.[8] He suggests, for example, an evolutionary trajectory of "Christendom-become-Western Civilization-now-becoming-Global Civilization."[9]

Most expositions of a global ethic subscribe to one or another ver-sion of a desacralized natural law or universal reason. For Küng, this means that the Declaration "should be formulated in such a way that phi-losophers—and indeed also agnostics and atheists—could accept it, even if they did not share the transcendent ground of such a declaration" (57). For his part, Swidler is even more explicit:

> We must build our theological language, categories, and images on our humanity, which we all—the traditional Jew, Christian, Muslim, the modern critical thinker, Hindu, Buddhist, Marxist—share in common. To the extent that we can formulate our reli-gious and ideological insights in such humanity-based language, we will be building a "universal theology of religion-ideology." In other words, we must attempt to cast our religious and ideologi-cal insights in language "from below," from our humanity, rather than "from above," from the perspective of the transcendent or the divine. We must attempt to develop a theological language "from within," not "from without." We must try to speak a lan-guage of immanence, not of transcendence . . . This new theologi-cal language might be called a theological-ideological Esperanto, for like Esperanto, it is intended as an intercultural language that borrows from various living languages. But it is so simplified, so rational, so generally human, that anybody with the knowledge of

8. Swidler, "Toward a Universal Declaration," 340.

9. Ibid., 338.

one's native tongue and a slight smattering of others will easily be able to master it.[10]

In analyzing this quote, Paeth notes that for some people—most notably Jeffrey Stout in *Ethics After Babel*—Esperanto is the wrong metaphor, decidedly inferior to a more ad hoc practice Stout calls a "socioethical form of Creole."[11]

On its own terms, the Global Ethic seems unlikely to bear even minimal weight across cultures and traditions in our "global" world. Its discovery of an already existing "commitment to a culture of non-violence and respect for life" doesn't even make it past the next page of the Declaration without being heavily qualified. It calls for powerholders to "commit themselves to the most non-violent, peaceful solutions possible" while embracing "an international order of peace which itself has need of protection and defence against perpetrators of violence" (25). So much for nonviolence. Similarly, "respect for life" operates at a high level of generality and nonspecificity that dares not speak of things like abortion or euthanasia or the weeding out of the physically or mentally disabled. Equivocation on the one hand, avoidance on the other—such typifies this worldwide commitment to nonviolence and respect for life, derived by a reason without place or particularity.

Similarly, the Global Ethic confuses its "is" and "ought" categories when it discerns a "commitment to a culture of equal rights and partnership between men and women." One wonders whether sufficient Muslims worldwide—not to mention the nearly half-billion Pentecostal Christians—would understand as do the Declaration's authors "the duty to resist wherever the domination of one sex over the other . . . even if in the name of religious conviction" (37). It will not do to treat words as empty receptacles filled incommensurably by various groups, and claiming "agreement" by virtue of having identical labels on such incommensurables.

In like fashion, the Delcaration claims that "In the great ancient religions and ethical traditions of humankind we find the directive: *You shall not commit sexual immorality! Or in positive terms: Respect and love one another!*" (32).

How much anguish our Anglican brothers and sisters might have been spared in recent years had they only had recourse to this wisdom—a

10. Swidler, *After the Absolute*, 56; quoted in Paeth, "Shared Values," 420.

11. Paeth, "Shared Values," 420.

global commitment to avoiding sexual immorality (no need to define that term, apparently) and loving one another (in what ways?) already existed, but the Anglicans apparently overlooked it. No matter—if Anglicans cannot discern the global consensus that makes self-evident the meaning of "sexual immorality," presumably groups like Muslims and neopagans will have an easier time specifying and embracing this already existing consensus.

God and Globalization

If the hope of the Global Ethic project—implicit in Küng, explicit in Swidler and others—is to construct a new sort of rationality not dependent on the particularities of any given religious tradition, then the God and Globalization project takes another approach. The latter suggests that the particularities of the Christian tradition (when properly understood) can underwrite ethical sensibilities sufficient to garner assent across religious traditions as part of attempts to guide and shape the direction of globalizing processes and institutions.

Among the many initiatives that aspire to a leadership role in scholarly discussions on this topic, God and Globalization deserves attention for several reasons. First, it has the backing of a significant institutional actor whose support made possible the convening of twenty scholars from around the world (Stackhouse rather proudly describes this as "one of the finest teams of Christian scholars ever assembled"[12]). The four volumes produced by the God and Globalization project presents a broad yet coherent exploration of a variety of issues and dynamics, and their presence in seminary and university libraries worldwide may give the project staying power over time.

At the same time, this project may be important beyond the confines of the Reformed theological tradition—indeed, as Stackhouse correctly notes, there is something of a convergence occurring among many mainstream Reformed and Catholic scholars in how they understand the relation of reason, revelation, and ethics. Both are committed to the notion of public theology, and both claim to speak to and for extra-ecclesial audiences with a language open to all via natural law or common grace. And God and Globalization may be disproportionately significant to the

---

12. Stackhouse, "General Introduction," 1.

extent that it legitimates some interpretations of globalization while marginalizing others: this may well garner friends for the initiative beyond the confines of church and academy (among corporate and governmental actors, for example).

Describing the God and Globalization project is simultaneously simple and difficult. It aims to use biblical categories (e.g., the Principalities and Powers) to fashion a complex model that attempts to illustrate the relations among a variety of global systems, the institutions and actors that operate within and across such systems, and the political, economic, cultural, and social/religious ideas that are both cause and consequence of globalization. Topics addressed by Stackhouse and his contributors include large-gauge considerations of transnational systems of economics, culture, and politics; institutional and professional exemplifications of law, medicine, science, and ecology; and Christian reflections on other religions. One of the frustrations awaiting those who engage all four volumes concerns the complex intellectual scaffolding in which Stackhouse invests so much—one that ultimately collapses under the weight of inconsistently employed terminology, confused or confusing notions of causality, and jargon and typology passed off as scholarly rigor.

God and Globalization builds its typological apparatus on top of the following assumptions:

- Every civilization, including the emerging global one Stackhouse sees drawing near, has religion of some sort at its core, from which religious ideas exercise influence on the general and particular character of that civilization.

- Religion operates best, now and in the global future, when it sees its arena and location as part of civil society—that realm of free association above the individual but outside the state. Civil society is "more determinative of and normatively more important for politics than politics is for society and religion."[13]

- The power of religion operating in the free arena of civil society resides in its ability to affect the institutions, rules, and spheres that reflect and empower globalization. This is done in many ways, but especially by creating an appropriate "ethos," which he defines as a "subtle web of 'values' and 'norms,' the obligations, virtues,

13. Stackhouse, "Civil Religion," 285.

convictions, mores, purposes, expectations, and legitimations that constitute the operating norms of a culture in relation to a social entity or set of practices."[14]

- Not every religious tradition, nor every tradition within the great religious traditions, can or should be allowed to shape ideas about life in a globalizing world. As Stackhouse says, "all operating values and norms, all examples of ethics as carried by institutions, cultures, societies, or civilizations, are not equal and . . . it is possible, even if difficult, to recognize the differences between authentic and inauthentic meanings, values, virtues, principles, goals and ends in organized bodies."[15] Anticipating the matter of *whose* standards ought obtain in relation to the above, Stackhouse gives his only mention in Volume One of Alasdair MacIntyre—dismissing him in a one-paragraph footnote by referring to "the Leninist and Nietzschian roots of his views."[16]

- God and Globalization, as articulated by Stackhouse, claims to be uninterested in a least-common-denominator understanding of religion and religious ethics (although it seems unlikely it can escape recourse to some version of it). The category of religion, the driving motor of civilizations past and future, is defined by Stackhouse as

  > one of the indispensable features of the common life: "religions" are the attempt to identify and cultivate life in response to the finding and commissioning Creative Power, variously conveyed and understood through symbols of transcendence, by which life, meaning, and morality are ultimately sustained; and "theological ethics" is an indispensable discipline by which a critical, publicly accessible discussion about the normative importance of key interpretations of the Creative Power can take place.[17]

- And finally, as noted previously, God and Globalization assumes that being able to be the prime mover of globalization is a competitive enterprise. Stackhouse and his colleagues are staking their claim to

14. Stackhouse, "General Introduction," 10.
15. Ibid., 11.
16. Ibid., 12.
17. Ibid., 38.

be the definitive spokespersons for "Christianity" in this process, or at least dictating the terms by which other would-be players must abide. Some ideas and traditions shouldn't be allowed a serious hearing, although those willing to conform to the disciplining criteria of public theology and its notion of reasoned discourse are welcome to contribute to the process. Christianity, if it does not squander the opportunity, is well placed to play a central role in shaping the future of globalization, and this for two reasons: the primary institutions, norms, and structures of globalization emerged from Christian cultures and norms (but don't dare call globalization a Western imposition); and in those Christian traditions steeped in covenant, incarnationalism, and common grace/natural law, it is possible to play a leading role in shaping global civil society without appearing to be dominative, neocolonial, or parochial. Shaping the global ethos along Christian lines understood in this fashion and by the reasoned practices of public theology, further, allows for the appearance of more open interaction with non-Christian traditions, free of the burdens of sectarianism.

While Küng's Global Ethic project seeks to find language deeper (or more shallow) than Christianity to discover and build amity among religions, Stackhouse enlists a coterie of collaborators to protect against some forms of Christian reason in order to facilitate a process of globalization with some specific features. And as it happens, policing the range of Christian discourse is materially related to the preferred outcomes of globalization—in this sense, they exemplify the sort of subservience of truthful reasoning to power explored by D. Stephen Long in *Speaking of God: Theology, Language, Truth*. The point of God and Globalization, seen from this vantage, seems to be about engineering a discourse that protects globalization from the charge that it is an ideological defense of rapacious capitalism. It also enables people to "know something about what is holy, and recognize that holy possibilities are not entirely absent from globalization."[18] In so doing, God and Globalization argues for a determinate theological method and its accompanying school of social analysis, which together make for a seamless and self-justifying theological and analytical system. I am speaking of the union between neo-Kuyperian "sphere sovereignty" in social ethics and functionalist social science as

18. Ibid., 5–6.

articulated by Talcott Parsons and his successors. The complex architecture of *God and Globalization*—its ambitious but sometimes frustrating framework of principalities, regencies, authorities, and the like—is an exercise in how to think about institutions, professions, networks, ideas, and cultures in ways that put sphere sovereignty at the center (and seems reminiscent of structural-functionalism during its heyday in the years after 1945).

The functionally distinct spheres—politics, economics, morality, and culture, and the like—obtain in all human communities (according to functionalism), and each has its own God-given authority and relative autonomy (according to Kuyperian social ethics). To the significant epistemically conservative bias of functionalism (what exists almost always performs some socially necessary purpose, otherwise it wouldn't have come into being and persisted), Kuyperianism adds a theological conservatism by way of a vocational theology that blesses conformity to role requirements specific to functionally defined spheres, requirements themselves that are defined independently of Christocentric or ecclesial categories.

In all of this talk of spheres and systems, there is an unavoidable ambiguity that works to subordinate discourse to predetermined acceptable outcomes. One the one hand, spheres are and should be relatively distinct and cohesive; on the other hand, what happens in one sphere should affect the functioning of other spheres. Stackhouse claims that only totalitarian systems try "to make spheres into fully closed systems"[19]—an impossible aim, even more so under conditions of global mobility. What sort of effects or interactions across spheres are normal and salutary, and what ones are inappropriate or dysfunctional, and hence to be resisted? While such is obviously complex and contextual, one area in which it is simple and straightforward is in seeing capitalism as a practically and theologically privileged system (or sphere) in Stackhouse's world. In fact, sphere sovereignty and functionalism combine to create something of a shell game that hides capitalism from serious criticism—seen in *God and Globalization*, but even more clearly in the work of Stackhouse's colleague Michael Novak. For them, whatever ills seem to flow from capitalism are more often created by other spheres and not the economic one (don't look there, look here, says the shell game barker). Any criticism or action opposed to

19. Ibid., 39–40.

55

capitalism is by definition an inappropriate infringement on the sovereignty of the economic sphere, and contrary to the social harmonization blessed by God as discerned by natural law and common grace.[20] Capitalism remains ever protected, and criticism of capitalism becomes a sinful violation of sphere sovereignty by definition. The power of religion—or, as Stackhouse calls it, the Creative Power—resides in its being "that which holds the whole together; it is decisive for shaping the ethos by which the spheres of society may cohere with one another and become coherent internally, both morally and spiritually."[21]

The irony in all of this, of course, is that while God and Globalization seeks and sees itself as more significantly "Christian" in its reasoning than the Global Ethic project, the operant rationality of the former shares much with the latter, perhaps to the dismay of both. Jesuit theologian John Coleman notes that the Bishops' Conferences of the European Community commissioned a report on global governance from former IMF Managing Director Michel Camdessus; in his recommendations on how to shape and govern the processes of globalization, Camdessus endorses the need for a global ethic and utilizes the same sort of reasoning present in the Global Ethic document—once again showing the political imperatives to which "intercultural ethics" must bend (in this case, a version of the future that puts capitalism beyond serious critique or challenge).[22] What the Global Ethic and God and Globalization projects share may be most apparent in what they drop from their reasoned discourse, whether aiming toward a common global ethic or constructing a moral ethos from broadly Christian categories capable of guiding globalization in preferred directions. What are omitted, at a minimum, are matters that may likely be building blocks for constructing an alternative interaction of reason and revelation to that offered by Kantianism and Kuyperianism.

It isn't clear how to say afresh what has been said so often about Christian ethics done with these emphases, but apparently it needs to be said yet again: that the particularities of revelation as exemplified in the practices, priorities, and dispositions of Jesus as recounted in the Gospels have no place in the "reasoned" discourses of Küng's or Stackhouse's approaches to social ethics. Avoiding these particularities remains central to

---

20. See Novak, *Spirit of Democratic Capitalism.*

21. Stackhouse, "General Introduction," 40–41.

22. Coleman, "Globalization," 178.

God and Globalization, to its ambitions to consolidate and lead Christian (and later non-Christian) thought and action across a wide array of concerns, and to concomitant domestication of eschatology and ecclesiology. Küng and his colleagues in the Parliament of World Religions make no claim to be doing Christian ethics except at some remove; but for God and Globalization, reason and revelation meet in ways that bleach out Jesus as both method and content for doing Christian ethics. Such will not do, in my view.

In over four volumes on globalization and Christianity, it is stunning that this project devotes no serious attention to the globalization of the Church itself; while the list of contributors is suitably multinational, no one explores the worldwide transformation of Christianity and what it might suggest about how to think about the globalization of politics, economics, culture, and the like. God and Globalization can't really do that, however, having already consigned the Church to the amorphous realm of civil society—along with flower clubs, bird fanciers, and nonprofit organizations of various sorts. Along with a growing list of theologians and other scholars, I think that consigning the worldwide body of Christ to the realm of civil society represents a significant category error. Further, that civil society stands largely free from the powers of state and market— a key assumption for God and Globalization, as too the assumption that spheres are actually "sovereign" in Kuyperian social ethics—seems either naïve or willfully blind to the immense power of political and economic phenomena to create and shape civil society, using everything from tax laws and regulatory regimes to the criminal code and the formation of affections and desires in many ways. The Church is not a subset of civil society, but it is a transnational body with a unique set of ends and— when it keeps discipleship as following Jesus at its center—a notion of "reasonable" action and discourse commensurate with those ends, ends not shared by any other actor in civil society (or the state).

As a side note, it is also worth noting that persons outside of theology have begun to raise concerns about the endless enthusiasms of our time with regard to "civil society." Writing in *Foreign Policy*, for example, Thomas Carothers notes that:

> Civil society has become one of the favorite buzzwords among the global chattering classes, touted by presidents and political scientists as the key to political, economic, and societal success.

> As with Internet stocks, however, civil society's worth as a concept
> has soared far beyond its demonstrated returns.[23]

While civil society is a "warm and fuzzy" term, Carothers notes, choosing
to embrace it with the enthusiasm shown thus far "depends on whether
you like snuggling up to the Russian mafia and militia groups from Mon-
tana as well as to your local parent-teacher association."[24]

THE CLASH OF CIVILIZATIONS

It isn't often that an article in a policy journal leads to a book, then to
an academic sub-industry all its own, then to what looks like a defining
aspect of international policymaking. Such has been the fate, however, of
the "clash of civilizations," a phrase popularized by the late MIT political
scientist Samuel Huntington in 1993 to describe the likely cleavages and
conflicts in the post-Cold War era, now more commonly used to mean
Islam against the West.

At the beginning, it was not entirely clear what Huntington meant by
some of his key terms, nor whether his understanding of them was necessarily the best or most helpful, nor whether the predictions he made were
inevitable or perhaps of the self-fulfilling variety.

In his 1998 book, *The Clash of Civilizations*, Huntington defined a
civilization as

> the highest cultural grouping of people and the broadest level of
> cultural identity people have short of that which distinguishes
> humans from other species. It is defined both by common objec-
> tive elements, such as language, history, religion, customs, institu-
> tions, and by the subjective self-identification of people. . . . The
> civilization to which [a person] belongs is the broadest level of
> identification with which he strongly identifies. Civilizations are
> the biggest "we" within which we feel culturally at home as distin-
> guished from all other "thems" out there."[25]

In the era after the Cold War, and as a result of dislocations caused
by economic globalization, Huntington claims that nation-states have
sorted themselves into affinity groups and alliances based upon cultural

23. Carothers, "Civil Society," 18.
24. Ibid., 20.
25. Huntington, *Clash of Civilizations*, 43.

similarity and sympathy. He identifies several separate civilizations (Hindu, Sinic/Chinese, Japanese, Islamic, Orthodox, Western). Sub-Saharan Africa may or may not constitute a civilization—Huntington thinks not, for the most part. Latin America is a curious case in Huntington's world, perhaps a subset of the West or a separate civilization of its own; Latin America might not be sufficiently Western, in his view, because it is more indigenous and too Catholic—the latter comes back to play later in Huntington's formulation in ways that should provide some cautions to the Church in a variety of social engagements.

Many scholars have criticized one or another aspect of Huntington's argument: his notion of civilization is too broad and too vague; there is as much conflict within cultures as between them; that he pays insufficient attention to conventional matters of political and economic conflict in shaping world affairs; and that the sort of policies that flow from such an imprecise theory may invite the very problems they are meant to address—that is, if you believe there's a fundamental and radical conflict between the West and world Islam, then you're likely to get one (which is one reason why the clash of civilizations rhetoric has been adopted wholesale by Al Qaida and other groups hoping to foment such a worldwide conflict).

The mileage this concept has enjoyed derives in no small measure because it has an intuitive appeal and doesn't easily admit of falsification. That there is violence in some parts of the world driven by people who claim to be fighting for a renewed Muslim *umma*, or worldwide community, is undeniable; that people care about more than just material interests, that ideas and culture matter, is similarly hard to refute. But to wrap them up all together and claim to have explained the driving engine of world conflict in our day and into tomorrow is a much more debatable proposition. That has not stopped it from finding its way into high-level discourse and policymaking—see President Bush's October 5, 2005, speech for one, in which Bush renamed it as a "clash of ideologies" for political purposes. The framework has also found favor among some conservative Catholics in Western Europe, perhaps looking for a rallying cause in the face of church decline and rising numbers of Muslim immigrants.

While the strengths and weaknesses of Huntington's argument have generated much attention, less scrutiny has been given to his assumptions about Catholicism in the world—a topic that he gives greater attention to in work before and after *The Clash of Civilizations*. While ecclesial solidarity is not an exclusively Catholic notion, Huntington's understanding of Catholicism is instructive in revealing the subordination of religion inherent in the "clash of civilizations," despite religion's presumed centrality to the very idea of civilization.

The Clash of Civilizations left open a number of questions of importance to Christians with a robust notion of ecclesiology. Huntington argued there that civilizations usually had a core state as a unifying and leading power, that these states usually had a dominant, unifying religion, and that what looked like statecraft may in fact be religious conflict by other means.

But where to fit the Catholic Church in all of that? Huntington's treatment makes situating Catholicism a difficult matter. Roman Catholicism is transnational, and certainly crucial to the development of the West—but it has also been important in the evolution of Latin America, which Huntington isn't sure counts as "the West." Catholicism has been important in sub-Saharan Africa, with dramatic numerical growth in the past century, but Huntington doesn't think that "Africa" counts as a civilization in its own right—he doesn't know where to put it, but he doesn't want to put it on a par with the West, China, or Japan. If one looks at a more generic category—Christianity, and not merely Catholicism—then why is Orthodoxy its own civilization while Catholicism or Protestantism is not? Where does the United States fit in all of this, an historically Protestant country whose single largest religious community is the Catholics, whose new migrants are overwhelmingly Christian and mostly Catholic?

Fortunately for us, Huntington wrote another book: *Who Are We? The Challenges to American National Identity*, which situates the United States and questions of culture, migration, religion, and identity within the "clash of civilizations" framework. It's an enlightening, almost surprisingly honest, explication of what this worldview means, how it positions Christianity in general and the Catholic Church in particular, and what's at stake if this set of explanations of culture, politics, and the world increases in currency.

There, Huntington spells out precisely what he thinks is the appropriate culture for "the West," as exemplified in the United States as leader of Western civilization in its conflicts with global Islam and China. Specifically, only a proper "Anglo-Protestantism" will do, one that harnesses religious commitment to the imperatives of nationalism and patriotism. What troubles Huntington so much about contemporary American culture lies in high rates of immigration from Mexico—these immigrants refuse to let go of their prior religious and cultural roots, resist assimilation into Anglo-Protestant ideas and practices, and threaten the national unity necessary to sustain the American project in a world of conflict and competition. If they refuse to Americanize and Protestantize (which can be done within mainstream Catholicism, as Huntington seems to understand and which others have stated more explicitly), then Mexicans should be forcibly excluded in the interest of national security, indeed for the welfare of "the West" as a whole.

Here's how he puts it:

> Protestant beliefs, values, and assumptions . . . had been the core element, along with the English language, of America's settler culture, and that culture continued to pervade and shape American life, society, and thought as the proportion of Protestants declined. Because they are central to American culture, Protestant values deeply influenced Catholicism and other religions in America. They have shaped American attitudes toward private and public morality, economic activity, government, and public policy. Most importantly, they are the primary sources of the American Creed, the ostensibly secular political principles that supplement Anglo-Protestant culture as the critical defining element of what it means to be American.[26]

Huntington looks favorably upon the privatization and individualization of Catholicism in the United States since the 1950s, a sign that it has become domesticated sufficiently to participate in Anglo-Protestant culture after years of being suspect and foreign. In some ways, his is a more respectable reading of longstanding American anti-Catholicism: Catholicism instills obedience to an external power, its concentration on sacramentalism renders its adherence poor candidates for rationality, its sense of the transcendent undermines the work ethic in the here and now, and so on. In fact, the story of anti-Catholicism has a happy ending for Huntington, as American Catholicism has been so completely domesticated as to be harmless to American political and worldwide aspirations. As he says:

> For more than two hundred years Americans defined their identity in opposition to Catholicism. The Catholic other was first

---

26. Huntington, *Who Are We?*, 62.

> fought and excluded and then opposed and discriminated against. Eventually, however, American Catholicism assimilated many of the features of its Protestant environment and was, in turn, assimilated into the American mainstream. These processes changed America from a Protestant country into a Christian country with Protestant values.[27]
>
> Catholics are proud of their American identity, the Americanization of their church, and its emergence as a central and influential institution of American society. For understandable reasons, however, they do not like people referring to the "Protestantization" of their religion. Yet in some degree that is precisely what Americanization involves.[28]

This is precisely why Huntington is so anxious about present immigration patterns—Mexicans migrating to the United States in large numbers are too Catholic for him, they are too attached to Mexican culture, they don't adopt American nationalist ideology deeply enough, and they speak Spanish instead of having come already fluent in English or committed to learning it at their earliest possible opportunity.

Keep in mind what is at stake here, in the "clash of civilizations" world—not just culture in the United States, but the health and vitality of the U.S. as the core nation-state of the West; not just whether political elites in the U.S. can count on public support for their programs, but whether the West will have the resolve, the unity, the faith—in what?—to stand against Islam and China and any other rival civilizations that threaten to topple Western supremacy. This truly is a cosmic struggle, one threatened from within by too many people with pictures of Our Lady of Guadaloupe in their homes and ties to family in their home villages. If they won't become self-respecting Anglo-Protestants (apparently Huntington hasn't heard about Pentecostal defections from Catholicism), if the U.S. Catholic Church can't make good Americans out of them as defined by people like Huntington, then they must be excluded, whether they intend to relocate legally or illegally. When you're fighting a clash of civilizations, churches must be mobilized or at least loyal, or else they're the enemy.

There is a comparable collision between Catholicism—remember, now a movement worldwide of poor people living outside Europe and North America—and the "clash of civilizations" idea in Europe.

27. Ibid., 92.
28. Ibid., 96.

One illustration of this comes from the pen of an internationally renowned journalist and author, famed for her fearless interviews with war criminals, dictators, and statesmen—people like Henry Kissinger, the Ayatollah Khomeini, and more. Her name is Oriana Fallaci, and having made her name as a mostly leftist intellectual in the 1960s, by her death in 2006 she had emerged as among the most provocative advocates of the "clash of civilizations" in a Europe with Muslim minorities in France, Germany, Italy, and elsewhere.

Reading Fallaci in her later days is not easy: her rhetoric is deliberately degrading and inflammatory, her accusations of disloyalty—to country, to reason, to the West—are venomous in the extreme. Of Muslims in Europe, she says, "They breed like rats."[29] Having moved to Europe in large numbers, Fallaci argues that "Muslims always come only to take. Only to plunder."[30] She accuses European politicians of treason, European intellectuals of hypocrisy, and the Catholic Church of having sold out the continent in the interests of cultural diversity and tolerance.

Her attacks on the Church are ironic at best, bizarre at worst. For Fallaci continued to proclaim herself, loudly and to whomever would listen, as a fanatical atheist, one for whom the idea of Abraham's god is appalling, for whom "turning the other cheek" is repellent. Yet much of her blame for the takeover of Europe by Islam—creating what she and some others call "Eurabia"—falls on the Church for not having been militant in opposing the invasion of the barbarians. She excoriates

> a Catholic Church which in the name of ecumenism has built the industry of pity. Because it is the Catholic associations which administer State benefits to immigrants. It is the Catholic associations which oppose their expulsions. Even when they are caught with explosives or drugs. It is The Catholic associations which grant them political asylum: the new tool of invasion.[31]

A curious combination, at first glance—a vigorous repudiation of Christianity and its ideas about God, along with an insistence that Christianity must define and defend what it means to be European and civilized. She claims that her atheism flows from "the very essence of Life," in which creatures eat one another to survive:

29. Fallaci, *Force of Reason*, 57.
30. Ibid., 115.
31. Ibid., 153.

> My atheism stems mainly from [this]. That is, from my refusal to
> accept the idea of a Creator who invented a world where Life kills
> Life, where Life eats Life. A world where in order to survive one
> has to kill and eat other living beings . . . If such an existence has
> been conceived by a Creator, I say, that Creator would be a very
> nasty one indeed.[32]

On the other hand, this view of life that she supposedly repudiates as
the creation of a Creator unworthy of belief and worship shapes much of
her view of politics, religion, and ethics. She castigates the peacemaking
emphases in Catholicism as contrary to Jesus and as hypocritical given the
Church's embrace of war for centuries[33]; in case anyone missed the point,
she asserts:

> I don't either believe in the masochism of turning the other cheek
> . . . I fight, I make war, I fight . . . [M]y war is right. Legitimate, du-
> tiful, right. And it is not true that all wars are wrong. Sometimes
> they are right. Legitimate, dutiful, right.[34]

Bishops and other church leaders who seek improved relations with Muslims are fools or traitors, the Church is traitorous to the cause of European
civilization and its survival, and along with the secular Left and Right, the
Church is part of a Triple Alliance that aids and abets the Islamic invasion
of Europe.

This self-described "Christian atheist" whose list of what she despises
includes churches, dogmas, liturgies, presumed spiritual authority, clerics,
material power, and especially the Christian idea of forgiveness, nonetheless sees Christianity as the cultural root of all she likes in European
cultural history. She even sees herself as comparable to Jesus of Nazareth,
whom she sees as rejected for speaking unpopular truths in his time (just
as she has been)[35]; like him, she sees herself as abandoned by her culture
and put on the Way of the Cross.[36]

What makes Fallaci something more than an intemperate, even
pathetic figure, is the extent to which her impassioned lament has reso-
nated with some Church figures even as they distance themselves from

32. Ibid., 23.

33. Ibid., 19.

34. Ibid., 23–24.

35. Ibid., 185–87, 190–91.

36. Ibid., 247.

her atheism and resolute anti-religious sensibilities. Fallaci's life and legacy drew a large audience during the 2007 meeting of Communion and Liberation in Rimini, Italy; Bishop Rino Fisichella, rector of the Lateran University in Rome and a friend of Pope Benedict XVI, described his friendship and relationship with Fallaci during the last years of her life. Fisichella described his relationship with her as a pastoral matter even as he underscored the significance of her outlook:

> [I]n her last years, radically and with deep conviction, she defended the idea that this country [Italy] belongs to the West. She defended like few others the profoundly Christian roots of the civilization to which we all belong, including the faith that, let's not forget, God forever offers to us as a great gift. We have to remember this woman for what she did, for what she said and wrote. She was a great woman, a great Italian, she deserves to be viewed with respect, and who now belongs to the history books.[37]

Journalist John Allen reported that Bishop Fisichella's remarks drew a "sustained standing ovation" from those in attendance—which suggests that, in addition to secularists like Fallaci who see Christianity as vested in the active defense of Western civilization, there are more than a handful of Christians for whom their faith ought to serve the preservation of their culture (even if that culture has become indifferent or hostile to the faith itself).

It is no surprise that for Fallaci and Huntington and others, the metaphor of "invasion" looms large in the threat to the West. It is one Catholics in the United States have heard used against themselves for a long time—they breed like rabbits (or rats, if you're Fallaci), they will replace decent values with ignorance and barbarism. For Fallaci, the Islamic takeover of Europe is part of a deliberate demographic strategy, openly discussed in Muslim circles, that she says is "a design based on gradual penetration rather than brutal and sudden aggression against the infidel-dogs and the bitch-dogs of the planet."[38]

Huntington, more temperate in his rhetoric, nonetheless sees in Mexican migration to the United States a demographic reconquista of lands taken from Mexico by the U.S. military—similar to the dreams of Islamists who hope to reconquer southern Spain by migration and breeding

37. Allen, "Deathbed Friendship."
38. Fallaci, *Force of Reason*, 126.

65

rates. Both are bad for the West, both are acts of war on the installment plan, and in both, the Catholic Church is a key player, for good or for evil. Either you fight for the West or you are a traitor—not merely to one's country, but to Western civilization in its entirety. Neutrality is not an option, multiple loyalties are not an option, and the gospel of peace is most definitely not an option. The instrumentalist view of Christianity displayed by Huntington and Fallaci—that it has social value to the extent that it serves the purposes of more important institutions and allegiances—could not be more clear, nor more at variance with an ecclesiology that takes the church and the Gospel seriously.

CHAPTER 4

National Identity:
Family, Nation, and Discipleship[1]

He was still speaking to the crowds when suddenly his mother and his brothers were standing outside and were anxious to have a word with him. But to the man who told him this Jesus replied, "Who is my mother? Who are my brothers?" And stretching out his hand toward his disciples he said, "Here are my mother and my brothers. Any one who does the will of my Father in heaven is my brother and sister and mother."

—Matt 12:46–50

INTRODUCTION

The quality of Christian reflection on matters of allegiance and discipleship is not helped by the degraded nature of public, secular discourse on controversial issues involving loyalty and nationalism. For-profit media conglomerates and low-rent populism alike put a premium on bombast and spectacle, punishing rather than rewarding the sort of careful and

1. A version of this was delivered as "Who Is My Mother? Family, Nation, Discipleship and Debates on Immigration," Scriptural Reasoning Section of the American Academy of Religion/Society for Biblical Literature National Meeting, November 20, 2006.

patient practices of reasoning needed for ecclesial discernment, and for interreligious dialogue across traditions.

A more helpful path forward might come via recourse to more communal reasoning practices grounded in scriptural interpretation and reflection. The contemporary renaissance in the theological interpretation of Scripture, enabling Christians to draw upon more ancient modes of scriptural engagement while mindful of the insights of contemporary scholarship,[2] may be useful in helping Christians think and speak on matters of allegiance and discipleship in ways that for the Church open questions and solutions not otherwise available in cultural debate.

With this in mind, I participated in a joint panel on "Scriptural Reasoning," sponsored by the American Academy of Religion, in 2006. We were asked to address the topic "Resident Aliens and the Ethics of Immigration"; Christian, Jewish, and Muslim scholars offered reflections on some aspects of their sacred texts as relevant to questions of migration.

With an assignment like this, many starting points presented themselves. At a minimum, it seemed apparent that "resident alien" status requires knowing how to be a good host and a good guest; it also presumes knowing who's the host, who's the guest, and who's responsible for what.

WHO'S WHO AND WHAT'S WHAT?

Christians in wealthy countries have all too easily assumed that for the most part these are "their" countries, that they are the powerful hosts, who are called upon to act benevolently toward the unfortunate. But what if Christians somehow relaxed the assumption that these are "our" countries, or that "our" country is our prime residence, or that national identity is the natural and logical manifestation of our earthly loyalties and allegiance—one that rests comfortably alongside that derived from membership in the worldwide body of Christ?

Notions of nationhood in general, and calls for exclusion in particular, at a deep level make strong assumptions concerning commonality, relatedness, and obligation. The civic republican tradition characteristically prides itself on being different—and hence superior to—more ethnically rooted notions of political community. For the former, commonality,

2. See for example Fowl, *Engaging Scripture*, and Fowl and Jones, *Reading in Communion*.

relatedness, and obligation are the fruits of shared commitments to democracy, liberalism, and the virtues of participation; for the latter, commonality, relatedness, and obligation are the products of more primordial ties of kinship, ethnicity, and cultural bonds.

As several scholars[3] note, the lines separating these traditions of analysis have always been more visible in the abstract than on the ground in advanced industrial societies. The European Union, for example, holds in an unstable balance ethnic-based notions of citizenship derived from Germany and purportedly more republican perspectives from France; in recent years, both positions have bent in reaction to one another and to the imperatives of EU expansion (toward the East) and exclusion (from the South).[4]

Political discourse in the United States has exhibited comparable tensions over the years, with republican and communal notions of commonality, relatedness, and obligation complementing or competing with one another. Despite the aspirations of republican voices, for whom "being an American" should remain open to whomever embraces the tenets of the American experiment, current debates are deeply infused with notions of political community as a natural entity whose integrity, stability, and sustainability are primary considerations. Republican notions inhabit metaphors strongly associational in character—citizenship, participation, and "those yearning to be free"—but all the while such ideas swim in a sea in which more powerful metaphors construct a world in which power is held by familial notions of belonging.

Many American commentators used to note the emotional depth and dangers attendant to national discourse built upon notions of family and nation, expressed in terms like "fatherland" or "motherland." Mothers and fathers, of course, derive their roles from establishing a home, and we are now neck-deep in the language of home in these matters—from Homeland Security to "domestic surveillance" and securing our "backyard," even reaching back nostalgically to celebrate earlier "bands of brothers" who protected the people from outside peril.

In this chapter, I hope to offer a Christian contribution to matters related to migration, borders, and nationalism by pursuing scriptural reasoning focused on the question of "the family." My contention, which for

3. See for example A. Marx, *Faith in Nation.*

4. For a comparative exploration, see Cesarani and Fulbrook, *Citizenship, Nationality and Migration.*

space reasons I can only assume rather than demonstrate, is that much policy and popular discourse on immigration, especially but not exclusively in its exclusionary expressions, presupposes a deep commitment to the notion of nation as family, of one's country as being like a family that defines the nature and limits of commonality, relatedness, and obligation.[5] While much well-intentioned religious activism employs scriptural proof-texting as ammunition in immigration policy debates, a more important—but perhaps more subversive—function may be to destabilize the presumed status of the family held dear both by restrictionists (protect the homeland) and advocates of more open-entry policies (based on the equal dignity of the "human family"). I hope to do this with an exploration of the family in the Gospel of Matthew.

AGAINST FAMILY VALUES

Once one enters the world of Matthew looking for insights into Jesus and the family, two things become apparent: there's a lot there, and one can never again accept the notion of Jesus as being "pro-family" in any conventional sense of the term. That the church has allowed itself to be seen as a defender of "family values" becomes, after a close reading of Matthew, one more instance of Christianity's attempt to hide its radical origins and trajectory. Given Matthew's deep engagement with the Judaism of the Jesus movement, the evangelist's subversion of the family may have implications for Jewish and Muslim reflections as well.

It is ironic, given what follows, that Matthew begins by establishing the familial bona fides of Jesus (1:1–17), and gives us much detail about the Holy Family before, during, and after the birth of Jesus (e.g., 1:18–25; 2:10–15; 2:19–23). John the Baptist throws the first stone at the presumed privilege of the family and lineage (3:8–10); the Spirit of God claims Jesus as His Son during Jesus' baptism in the Jordan (3:16–17); the devil himself first calls Jesus the Son of God (4:3); and Jesus first refers to God as his Father in teaching his disciples how to pray, giving them the "Our Father," or the Lord's Prayer (6:9–13).

Family language everywhere, but none of it prepares the reader or would-be follower for what is to come. Matthew gives a clue that something is off-kilter (8:21–22) when he puts following Jesus above the sacred obligation to bury one's own father; it is significant that this response is

5. For a current example, see Huntington, *Clash of Civilizations*.

to a question asked by a disciple, not just anyone, for it is the category of discipleship that Matthew's Jesus places over against and above the natural primacy of the family. In doing so, he lays dynamite at the foundation of the social order then and now, a move that persons inside and outside the Church have attempted to reverse ever since.

Most readers of Matthew identify the Sermon on the Mount, which includes the Beatitudes and other directives, as the part of the drama with the most radical implications. I would suggest that other sections are similarly charged for those with eyes to see—and these involve giving primacy to discipleship in matters of commonality, relatedness, and obligation, with a dramatic reduction in power to the family and (by extension) other primordial, "natural," and self-evident identities and communities. When Jesus takes on the biological family in the name of discipleship, he also shakes the "extended family" of the national state for Christians seeking to follow Jesus.

Matthew's tenth chapter instructs the apostles on their mission, authority and calling. Jesus here also warns them of the obstacles that await them, and the persecution that will greet them as a consequence of following him. Such will not be random in its sources, says Jesus; rather, "Brother will betray brother to death, and a father his child; children will come forward against their parents and have them put to death" (10:21). Later in that chapter, Matthew's Jesus harkens back to Micah (7:6) in identifying the family as a prime obstacle to the gospel. I wish everyone who has ever built a ministry, political program, or media empire on the claim that Christianity is "pro-family" would have to wear this bit of Matthew around their necks. I refer, of course, to Matt 10:34–39 (NRSV):

> Do not think that I have come to bring peace to the earth; I have not come to bring peace, but a sword.
>
>> For I have come to set a man against his father,
>> and a daughter against her mother,
>> and a daughter-in-law against her mother-in law;
>> and one's foes will be members of one's own household.
>
> Whoever loves father or mother more than me is not worthy of me; and whoever loves son or daughter more than me is not worthy of me; and whoever does not take up the cross and follow me is not worthy of me. Those who find their life will lose it, and those who lose their life for my sake will find it.

The family opposes discipleship in many ways, as Matthew and the other evangelists warn. It tempts one toward privileging blood relatives over all else, puts protecting family respectability and reputation above proclaiming the gospel, and counsels realism, practicality, and the safe path over the Way that may lead to exclusion, suffering, and martyrdom.

Matthew gives us ample evidence that the conflict between Jesus and family was well recognized in the narrative itself. He returns to his home town to teach in the temple, but instead of a hero's welcome he meets with rejection.

> [The people asked] "Where did the man get this wisdom and these miraculous powers? This is the carpenter's son, surely? Is not his mother the woman called Mary, and his brothers James and Joseph and Simon and Jude? His sisters, too, are they not all here with us? So where did this man get it all?" And they would not accept him. But Jesus said to them, "A prophet is despised only in his own country and in his own house," and he did not work many miracles there because of their lack of faith. (Matt 13:54–58)

Matthew demonstrates still another disconnect between discipleship and family loyalty when Jesus criticizes the mother of Zebedee's sons for doing what all mothers everywhere and at all times have done—namely, looking out for the welfare of their children, in this case trying to help them get a leg up in their career:

> Then the mother of Zebedee's sons came with her sons to make a request of him, and bowed low; and he said to her, "What is it you want?" She said to him, "Promise that these two sons of mine may sit one at your right hand and the other at your left in your kingdom." Jesus answered, "You do not know what you are asking. Can you drink the cup that I am going to drink?" They replied, "We can." He said to them, "Very well; you shall drink my cup; but as for seats at my right hand and my left, these are not mine to grant; they belong to those to whom they have been allotted by my Father." (Matt 20:20–23)

But Jesus doesn't stop here. In fact, he uses his destabilizing of family primacy to call into question other natural roles, allegiances, and responsibilities.

> When the other ten heard this they were indignant with the two brothers. But Jesus called them to him and said, "You know that

> among the gentiles the rulers lord it over them, and great men
> make their authority felt. Among you this is not to happen. No;
> anyone who wants to become great among you must be your ser-
> vant, and anyone who wants to be first among you must be your
> slave, just as the Son of man came not to be served but to serve,
> and to give his life as a ransom for many." (Matt 20:24–28)

In other words, not only must followers of Jesus put being a disciple over
being a good family person, this "being a disciple" may also render them
unsuitable for exercising power in the secular realm. How can a disciple
serve as a ruler, or even as a functionary in the ruler's apparatus, with
Jesus' notion of legitimate and illegitimate power and its exercise? However much worldly power cloaks itself in the soft language of service, its
institutions (consider the modern state and modern capitalism) presume
the indispensability of the sort of power that Jesus calls upon his disciples
to abjure.

FAMILY AND THE NATION AS HOME

Matthew on the family ought to make one forever suspicious of any sort
of theology that privileges so-called "natural" institutions—the family,
states, and the like—as among the self-evident goods to be embraced and
celebrated by the Church. Doing so has led to a host of developments
throughout Christian history at odds with the call to discipleship, developments that have placed other identities and allegiances above those a
Christian accepts at baptism into the community called to be herald and
foretaste of the Kingdom of God.

Inasmuch as the nation is among these "natural" entities presumed
to be good and valuable in and of themselves, and insofar as notions of
"natural" community, cohesiveness, and identity underwrite much mainstream debate on borders and movement, then Matthew's scriptural assault on the family may have something to say in reframing the entire
question for Christians and other interested people. For if even the family—an intricate and tangible source of identity—has value only and to
the extent that it serves the cause of discipleship, how much less claim
on Christian practices of commonality, relatedness, and obligation should
the modern nation-state enjoy?

If notions of citizenship based upon "natural" affinities and nation-as-family are undermined by this reading of discipleship, what of the civic republican tradition of commonality, obligation, and relatedness? With its roots in Aristotle, the civic republican tradition puts the polis above the family (unlike the ethnic-nationalist tradition, which sees the nation as the family writ large). My contention, which again for space considerations must be assumed rather than demonstrated, is that while Christian discipleship agrees that family is subordinated to polity, it disagrees with the Greeks on what the true polity is—not the state, but the community of disciples called the Church. Being a Christian ought to be the fundamental category of membership, constraining and disciplining for followers of Jesus civic claims of commonality, obligation, and relatedness.

SOME IMPLICATIONS

In a public culture that all too quickly collapses public discourse into public policy—what should the state do—it is not clear what implications, if any, flow from this sort of reading of Matthew and the family. I confess to not being troubled if this approach provides no immediate guidance to policymakers; better, in my view, if this reading offers alternative starting points for discussion for Christians and their fellow seekers after God's truth.

Still, if pressed, a few policy-related matters might derive from the preceding. For example:

1. One should consider de-emphasizing "citizenship" as the goal or prize to be won in order to be seen as a full member of "the nation" or "community." The blessing of God as conveyed through Jesus cannot be contained by the borders of polity or ethnicity: see for example, the daughter of the Canaanite woman healed despite being a non-Israelite "dog" (Matt 15:21–28), and the centurion whose faith surpassed that of Israel so much that Jesus exclaimed that "many will come from east to west and sit down with Abraham and Isaac and Jacob at the feast in the kingdom of Heaven" (Matt 8:5–13). Of course, when the kingdom of Heaven does arrive, with divine judgment upon "all nations" (the nations do not judge the Church, the saints, or their own conduct—they are not sovereign), the tests do not come with checks for passports, papers, or loyalty oaths:

For I was hungry and you gave me food, I was thirsty and you
gave me drink, I was a stranger and you made me welcome, lacking clothes and you clothed me, sick and you visited me, in prison
and you came to see me. (Matt 25:36–7)

Citizenship should be de-emphasized as the ultimate good because
of the idolatry implicit in the concept. It is not at all clear, for example, that
a Christian whose discipleship joins him or her to the worldwide body of
Christ could take the U.S. Citizenship oath in good conscience—especially if he or she is a Christian pacifist (or rigorous just-war proponent) in a
mainline Protestant or Catholic community. Nor should Christians look
approvingly upon those shortcuts to citizenship offered by state policies
that allow immigrants to "prove" their loyalty to the state by killing and
dying in the military.

2. Perhaps Christians should dare to raise the prospect of open immigration as something worth exploring.[6] While such a policy stance
stands no chance of adoption in my lifetime, short of a cataclysmic series of events, raising it might have an educative function for the following reason: The hubris of empire is that it demands to be welcomed as a
resident alien, and increasingly as a citizen, anywhere in the world, while
denying reciprocity to whomever it chooses. Under the present capitalist
dispensation, the United States demands the right to exclude labor (via re-
strictive immigration laws inhibiting the mobility of wage-earners) even
as it punishes countries that would presume to keep out American capital.

For the textbook picture of world economics to have even a ghost of
a chance of working (I find the textbook picture unpersuasive, but that is
for another time), one must have full-factor mobility, so that labor and
capital can move efficiently and smoothly to areas of maximal return and
benefit. Demanding it for capital while denying it for labor is the most
blatant form of a rigged game, where the rules are stacked against working people in favor of those who live off the past labor that we call capital
investment. Were Christians to call for open movement instead of restric-
tions on human flows, the hypocrisy of the existing order might usefully
be brought into view in ways presently obscured by the disjointed nature
of public discourse on capital liberalization and labor/human restriction.

3. Another set of policies, ecclesial more than governmental, may
emerge from taking seriously the aforementioned transnational nature of

6. See Laufer, *Wetback Nation*, for a recent exploration of the notion.

the Church—the Church being a more universal "polity" against which nations and states look positively sectarian, parochial, and tribal. When Catholic clergy and leaders in Mexico help undocumented people to cross into the United States, fleeing starvation or oppression, who am I as a fellow Christian to ignore their pleas for help in the name of Christian solidarity? When a woman driven by desperation attempts a desert crossing, protected by not much more than a picture of Saint Toribio Romo, patron saint of migrants, am I to hand her body over to the state in the name of civic republicanism or national community? I think not; I think a casual but consistent disregard for the imperatives of state may be the order of the day for those whose sense of commonality, relatedness, and obligation is neither familial nor civic, but ecclesial—sealed in the Resurrection that itself was a criminal offense against Roman law (Matt 27:63–66), and the border between the dead and the living.

CHAPTER 5

Border Crossings:
Immigration through an Ecclesiological Lens[1]

As most of you know, the political battle over immigration has spread from the federal to the state and local level in recent years. State legislatures, city and county governments, and more have proposed and sometimes passed laws on the subject—while a few, like the city of San Francisco, have declared themselves as "sanctuary" places, the majority of initiatives have been exclusionary in nature. In recent years, more than 1,100 pieces of legislation have been introduced in thirty-five states, with forty-four laws adopted in twenty-six states.

Among the most far-reaching sub-national initiatives has been that passed by the Oklahoma legislature, going into effect on November 1, 2008. This measure, introduced and known as House Bill 1804, makes it a felony to transport illegal immigrants knowingly, and creates new barriers to such immigrants being hired or receiving government services. When California considered a similar bill a few years ago, many of you may recall that several church leaders announced their refusal to comply with such laws if enacted—Los Angeles' Roger Cardinal Mahoney among them.

Such a law is now in place in Oklahoma, and it threatens to criminalize a range of church ministries and programs for undocumented persons.

1. A version of this was delivered as "Immigration and the Church," Grace Urban Ministries, San Francisco, CA, April 3–4, 2008.

One of the most remarkable developments to date, which I want to share with you today, is a pastoral letter written by Edward J. Slattery, the Catholic bishop of Tulsa in eastern Oklahoma. Only the second pastoral letter written by Slattery in his fourteen years in office, it is a remarkable illustration of what it might mean for the churches to chart their course on immigration by their own lights rather than those set by the state. One need not be Catholic to see the ecclesiological significance of Slattery's intervention; it's also worth noting that he's not known as an especially radical member of the church hierarchy.

Allow me to read from several sections of this letter. First, notice the authority by which he claims to speak, and to whom his words are addressed in the first instance:

> As a bishop, I speak with the voice of one who has been consecrated to proclaim the truth of the Gospel here in Eastern Oklahoma, and I do so with the authority and in the name of Jesus Christ, King of the Universe.
>
> I do wish to make it clear that I am writing this pastoral letter in the exercise of my pastoral mission for you, the People of God who have been confided to my care, for you are that community which I must teach, sanctify and govern with the authority and responsibility that I exercise in communion with the whole college of Bishops . . .[2]

Bishop Slattery finds his job description in the Scripture and history of the Church, expressed in Second Vatican Council in this way:

> For bishops are preachers of the faith who lead new disciples to Christ. They are authentic teachers, that is, teachers endowed with the authority of Christ, who preach to the people committed to them the faith they must believe and put into practice.[3]

Having quoted Vatican II on the duties of a bishop, Slattery describes the mandate of all ministers of the gospel:

> . . . when I preach the truth of the Gospel—independent of whether or not what I say corresponds with the laws of men and of civil societies—my words are guarded by that same Spirit Who anointed the Lord Jesus in the synagogue of Nazareth and filled Him with the power to *"preach good news to the poor . . . to set at*

2. Slattery, *Suffering Faces of the Poor*, 1.

3. *Lumen Gentium*, 25.

liberty those who are oppressed and to proclaim a year of favor from the Lord." (Luke 4:18–19)

Consecrated a bishop in service to the Lord Jesus Christ, I am as well a disciple and missionary of His Gospel.[4]

With this sense of responsibility, you get a fairly bold proclamation of the duty of a minister (and perhaps some wishful thinking about the responsibility of the faithful):

In this way, I wish to make it clear that I do not speak as an elected official, whose service to the public proceeds from the will of those who elected him or her to office. Nor do I speak as a civil servant, appointed to the task and accountable to those by whom he or she has been appointed. Rather, I speak as the Catholic Bishop of this Diocese and I speak with the authority of Jesus Christ, Who in His life here on earth always showed his predilection for the poor and the oppressed. Encouraged, then, by the certainty that you will listen to me as you would listen to Christ Himself *(Luke 10:16)* . . .[5]

Why all of this attention to role and authority, to mandate and leadership? Most pastoral letters by church leaders these days, in fact, are much more modest in tone, sometimes more akin to advice from an older sibling or one's greybearded uncle. The bishop of Tulsa starts this way—not arrogant, but not bashful either—I suspect, because he's preparing to tell the faithful things most of them are not going to want to hear.

And he does. Listen to his description of the new Oklahoma immigration law, HB 1804:

The basic intention of this law is to deny those who have entered our country illegally the right to work in Oklahoma and the right to find shelter for their families in our communities. Thus they are forced to flee our state. I believe that the right to earn one's living and the right to shelter one's family securely are basic human rights, the fundamental building blocks of a just society, and to deny these rights is immoral and unjust. I also believe that since the intention of HB 1804 is immoral, when it is implemented, the effects will be an intolerable increase in the suffering endured by

---

4. Slattery, *Suffering Faces of the Poor*, 2.
5. Ibid., 2–3.

the families of illegal immigrants, plus the spiritual suffering of those who must enforce it.

HB 1804 creates an atmosphere of repression and terror designed to make it impossible for those illegal immigrants who have settled here to find a stable, secure life for themselves and their children, many of whom are native born citizens with civil rights equal to our own.[6]

The Bishop then proceeds to discuss the need for an overhaul of national immigration practices, and the problems the new law will create. In light of the suffering and injustice this new law creates, how should the Church as Church respond?

Listen to Slattery as he grounds his church's path in the gospel and in Scripture:

I am a citizen of the United States. I love my nation and will follow the Constitution and the laws which govern us as a free society. But as a bishop of the Catholic Church, my life has been consecrated to the proclamation of the Gospel of Jesus Christ. I am to guard the Deposit of Faith and show Christ's love and compassion to the poor, to the strangers in our midst and to the disadvantaged. Above all else, I must be a good shepherd of the flock which Christ the Lord has placed under my care, this local Church which is established in Eastern Oklahoma where I have lived and served these past fourteen years and where eventually I hope to die and be buried.

The application of an anti-immigration law, whether it affects Catholics or non-Catholics, presents me—as the Catholic Bishop of this Diocese—with new challenges, to which I must respond with the "arms" spoken of by Saint Paul to the first Christians in Ephesus, those gifts which I believe God has given me for resistance against the day of evil, to remain firm, so that afterwards we may triumph in Christ: *Stand, therefore, having girded your loins with truth and having put on the breastplate of righteousness and having shod your feet with the equipment of the Gospel of peace; besides all these, taking the shield of faith with which you can quench all the flaming darts of the evil one. And take the helmet of salvation, and the sword of the Spirit which is the Word of God. Pray at all times in the spirit, with all prayer and supplication. To that end, keep alert with all perseverance, making supplication for all the holy ones, and also for me, that utterance may be given me in opening*

6. Ibid., 6.

my mouth boldly, to proclaim the mystery of the Gospel, for which I am an ambassador in chains. May I declare it boldly as I ought to speak. (Eph. 6:14–20).[7]

Given this, he tells the church,

> Our faith calls us to serve those in need with the same prompt response and the same generous love that we would show Christ Himself were He to come before us sick or tired or in need. To make charity a crime is to make those who love criminals . . . and when it becomes a crime to love the poor and serve their needs, then I will be the first to go to jail for this crime and I pray that every priest and every deacon in this diocese will have the courage to walk with me into that prison.[8]

To show that he's not interested in merely a symbolic sort of civil disobedience, a sort of choreographed trespassing arrest that leaves everyone happy and satisfied, Bishop Slattery then outlines a diocesan plan of action in response to HB 1804:

> In order that we might live out our commitment to the Gospel in unity and charity, I am going to propose the following as a Diocesan plan of action in response to the situation of fear created in so many of our neighbors by the implementation of HB 1804:
>
> • Equal accessibility to all Catholic Programs
>
> I wish to make it absolutely clear that no one will be denied access to our Catholic charitable, pastoral and/or educational programs because they are illegal immigrants. This is to be true for all our parishes, institutions, schools and the various operations of Catholic Charities.
>
> • Legal Resources
>
> We will do whatever we can to provide legal assistance through our Catholic Charities to those who need help in establishing or maintaining their legal residence in this country. We also implore those lawyers who have reasonable expertise in the field of immigration law to step forward and volunteer their services in the single most effective way we have of alleviating the suffering of our neighbors, parishioners and friends.

7. Ibid., 13–14.
8. Ibid., 14.

- Legal Documentation

  We will work with legal agencies to prepare a standardized "Power of Attorney" form which parents can use in case of emergency to indicate whom they want to assume guardianship over their dependent children should those parents be arrested and sent for deportation.

- Providing Catholic Foster Care

  When it happens that one or both parents are arrested and sent for deportation and some provision must be made for their dependent children, we will offer every resource for the protection and safety of these children. If the parents have indicated their intentions through a legal "power of attorney" form, we will do whatever we can to make certain that the parents' decision as to who is best suited to care for their children is respected. We will immediately begin a process of identifying and training families who can provide shelter for the children of illegal immigrants who have indicated that they would prefer the Church to assume responsibility for their children until such time as the family can be reunited. We will work with whatever government agencies we can to assist in the humane and compassionate rejoining of these children and their parents.[9]

Finally, and in the long run perhaps more importantly, Bishop Slattery has inserted a prayer to be said throughout his diocese at the end of every Sunday Mass. It is in two parts—a Marian petition subordinated to the second appeal, addressed to God the Father. Consider if you will the formative potential of this sort of prayer working its way into the affections, dispositions, and practices of Christians, as weeks turn into months, and months into years:

Let us pray:

Oh Father of Mercy, Your Only begotten Son suffered the threats of Herod and the pain of exile though just a child. Grant, we beseech you, courage and hope to immigrant families who sojourn in a land not their own and preserve them from every injustice. By your grace may we live in this world, so as to give witness that our citizenship is in heaven and our native home is the Kingdom

9. Ibid., 15–16.

of your Son, who lives and reigns with You and the Holy Spirit, one God, forever and ever. Amen.[10]

Quite a remarkable example, I would say, of the church being the church in season and out. Not a big political campaign, not a get-out-the-vote push, not even sit-ins at the capitol building—just the everyday life of the church: worshiping God, performing the corporal and spiritual works of mercy, setting pastoral priorities in accord with Matthew 25, and seeking justice for the marginalized.

I took the liberty of tracking some public comments on Bishop Slattery's pastoral letter. Here are some selections:

One said: "Lock up the Bishop—if he does not follow Federal and State Law—plan and simple!"

Another: "The Bishop is sticking his nose in the federal law. Lock him up!"

A third: "Ya know . . . he should keep his mouth shut. Everyone knows religious organizations are tax exempt. And while churches keep asking for donations and tithes, they don't have to pay taxes on any of that money. As such, he really should have nothing to say about this."

From another citizen: "If the church 'aids and abets' the illegals, they are breaking the law, and should be punished. Federal law has priority over the church. If any church doesn't recognize this, they need to be shut down."

From still another: "Gee, most of the illegal aliens are Catholic! That puts a dent in the collection plate, and they have a lot of priest abuse cases to pay off."

CHURCHES AS NATIONAL SECURITY PROBLEMS

For those of you working as part of the so-called New Sanctuary Movement, the church in the sights of the national security state is no surprise. What we may be seeing is an expansion of the definition of national security threats, a larger number of congregations under investigation and suspicion, and new attempts to divide and subvert congregational and ecclesial unity.

Some of you may have heard of John Fife, a Presbyterian pastor in Tucson, who during Reagan's proxy wars in Central America saw his

10. Ibid., 16.

congregation infiltrated by the FBI, wiretaps employed, and informants exploited. Fife was among the founders of the 1980s sanctuary movement, moving thousands of people fleeing political persecution to safe haven churches around the country. For defying federal law and the government's Cold War manipulation of international refugee and asylum codes (to which the U.S. was and is a signatory), Fife and his friends were convicted of several federal offenses.

The state's capacity to infiltrate and target churches has increased significantly since the 1980s—more expansive powers, more vectors to monitor (e-mail, instant messaging), no judicial push-back whatsoever. The U.S., like all modern states, does not recognize churches as "sanctuaries" or zones free of state control or sovereignty—raids or the lack thereof are political questions, not matters of jurisprudence or limits on state power. No one knows for sure how many churches, pastors, or communities are or have been under investigation, but the number is almost certain to grow in the years ahead.

In such an environment, it's also reasonable to expect state efforts to penetrate legal protections for clergy confidentiality—the confessional, counseling relationships, and the like. While in the short term such is likely to have focused on Muslim communities, things like the New Sanctuary Movement and the non-cooperative stances of persons like Bishop Slattery promise similar things for the churches. One can envision a common front on such issues, as happened last year in Australia when Christian, Jewish, and Muslim leaders issued a common policy on protecting clergy confidentiality.

Realistically, of course, we can expect frequent betrayals of ecclesial solidarity under pressure from national security and legal pressures. Given two interrelated factors—the generally weak formation of Christians and a correspondingly thin notion of the church as the primary allegiance of Christians, and the strength of nationalist formation and patriotic formation in the United States—one can expect clergy and laity alike to privilege state power over their congregations. The results will likely be significant but probably unavoidable.

There are a few terms and concepts you can expect to see with greater frequency should churches begin to put their baptismal vows over the claims of Caesar to define and confine the gospel.

The first of these is treason. While the more sophisticated use phrases like "philanthropic lawlessness,"[11] others are more direct. My favorite is Pastor Ralph Ovadal of Pilgrims Covenant Church in Wisconsin, who claims that "the Roman Catholic Church is aiding and abetting the criminal invasion of America by Mexicans."[12] There's an object lesson here for my non-Catholic Christian friends—should your sense of church lead you to stand for the alien and the stranger, you'll find yourselves branded as honorary Catholics. While we're glad to have you, I'm afraid it's not something you may enjoy if views like Pastor Ovadal's continue to gain in popularity. You'll be participating in what he and others describe as the "reconquista" of the United States by Mexico and the Vatican.

As he says:

> The Roman Catholic Church is determined to turn Protestant America into a Roman Catholic country, and her best bet to do that is to bring as many Catholics into our nation as possible . . . Plainly speaking, the goal is to eliminate America's security along our border with Mexico! The US bishops together with their Mexican counterparts, of course with papal consent and encouragement, have determined to use Catholic treasure, influence, and manpower to erase America's border. This is not surprising to the discerning Christian. Sovereign nations have always been a hindrance to the pope's effective exercise of his office as "father of kings, governors of the world, and Vicar of Christ."[13]

There are more polite versions of this general view, of course. CNN's Lou Dobbs thunders against churches who dare challenge immigration law, calling for repeal of tax-exempt status for those engaging in "politics."[14] Similarly, the restrictionist organization FAIR not-too-subtly reminds churches that they jeopardize billions of dollars in state and federal funds that flow to church-based social service organizations.[15] In ways such as these do cozy relations between churches and states in one era become shackles on the churches in another.

The Church has never been home only to martyrs and the brave, of course. Threats and inducements from governments have fractured

11. Levitske, "Illegal Immigration."
12. Ovodal, "Romanizing America."
13. Ibid.
14. Dobbs, "Lou Dobbs Tonight."
15. FAIR, "Morality of Mass Immigration."

Church unity in the past, and will do so again in the future. One interesting example that relates, in at least one sense, concerns recent revelations of Protestant, Catholic, and Orthodox clergy who collaborated with secret police forces in East Bloc countries during the Cold War (for discussion of this case, see chapter 10).

The point of raising this isn't to cast aspersions or issue easy judgments on persons in a different time and circumstance. It does invite speculation, however, on how similar practices by clergy and Church leaders would be received if done in the United States. Were clergy to inform on their members, or on one another—and immigration is a key and likely issue for such now and in the years ahead—I suspect the reaction here would be much more divided. On the one hand, turncoats have a low reputation in the United States—if they're called a "whistleblower," however, they are likely to be celebrated. Whereas at least some churches in Eastern Europe had no illusions about the legitimacy or virtues of the regimes in power, American Christians have been formed much more deeply in narratives that lionize the regime, that see it as virtuous, almost a sacred force in history. It's no stretch of imagination to envision Fox News and countless other media celebrating Church informants (with the FBI, ICE, Homeland Security and others) as the true defendants of Christianity against subversive Church elites who have temporarily hijacked Church bodies and positions. Such was precisely the rationale for those Latin American states whose death squads targeted Church leaders in the name of defending Christian values. And given the gap between clergy and lay views on issues like immigration, there is a serious division to be exploited unless the Church begins to take its own formation processes more seriously.

If you doubt that illegal immigration is the sort of issue that could lead to split and infiltrated congregations, it means that either you're part of an unusually unified congregation, or else you're not paying attention. Even a cursory glance at opinion poll data reveals significant gaps between leaders and laity on migration questions. This is true for mainline Protestants, non-Latino Catholics, evangelicals, and African-American Protestants. More than half of white evangelicals favor criminalizing assistance to undocumented immigrants, while half of mainline Protestants and Catholics hold the same view.[16] Fully half of all Americans, white and

16. Smith, "Attitudes Toward Immigration."

black, feel immigrants threaten American customs and values, a view held by 63 percent of white evangelicals (white evangelicals, mainline Protestants, and non-Latino Catholics comprise 60 percent of the American population).

Being Church for the Long Haul

There is an understandable tendency among Christians dealing with the immediacy of immigrants in this system—their vulnerability, their openness to abuse on all sides—to think primarily or exclusively in terms of public policy issues. The needs are manifest, so the answer must be to grab hold of the political levers, immerse oneself in advocacy and deal-making and lobbying. This instinct oftentimes makes all of this "church stuff" seem like a luxury, a self-centered "extra" that can be put aside in favor of another march, another lobbying campaign, another action plan.

I suggest to you that such should be resisted as not being in the best interest of those we help today and in the future. We do them and ourselves more good, paradoxically enough, when the Church stays true to its best self as the people commissioned by God to live the promises of Jesus. This means something other than making faith merely an instrumental fuel or motivation for the presumably more important work of secular politics, and it means something other than prioritizing policymaking in how the Church addresses immigration.

Privileging policymaking, lobbying, and the like raises a host of other issues not usually taken seriously enough in the churches. Policymaking is inevitably framed in terms of the national interest and national values, and how Christianity helps society think and act more adequately in those areas. It is not obvious, however, that the national interest or the health of the state should be the Church's priority, or that the Church should necessarily agree with the self-proclaimed interests and values of *any* state or society. One might ask, for example, whether the near-unanimous focus on achieving citizenship for undocumented persons reflects far more than an instrumental calculation (citizenship in one's country of residence provides certain protections from abusive behavior) and moves too easily into the quasi-idolatrous notion that love of country is the highest good, one which the Church is obliged to advance.

Immigration, like some other issues, admits of no policy package that will "solve" the problem—it is a structural problem deeply rooted in the workings of contemporary capitalism. There will continue to be many issues, crises, and outrages even if "comprehensive" immigration reform is implemented—for example, the incoherence and injustices attendant to the no-longer-plausible distinction between "economic migrants" and "political refugees."

In all of this, one has to wonder why, with so many people in the United States identifying themselves as Christians, the churches have had so little influence on questions like immigration. One reason, of course, is that most people in the pews are far more American than Christian—they have been formed more deeply by the narratives, stories, and symbols of nationalism than by the gospel. One of the major ecclesiological imperatives of our time may in fact derive from this circumstance—a renewed emphasis on "converting the baptized," if you will, a commitment to forming disciples rather than citizens, persons for whom "being a Christian" is the primary identity and loyalty that then orders and conditions lesser ones.

This will take different forms in our various traditions and church polities, of course, but a general failure of Christian formation seems to be an ecumenical bond of embarrassment—some do it less poorly than others, but few can claim with confidence that their members or their children are more deeply shaped by the Sermon on the Mount than by the identities, affections, and desires of non-Christian cultural forces.

At the same time, however, the ease with which people now move around the world promises to bring to the attention of the Church in North America some profound changes that are likely to change a great many things about being a Christian in the years ahead. I'm speaking about the unprecedented transformation of Christianity as a religious movement centered in Europe and North America to one whose majority is now found in the poor parts of the world—Latin America, Africa, and Asia. This so-called rise of "World Christianity" involves myriad transformations, from demographic changes and shifts in mission patterns (areas of growth and decline), to matters of worship, doctrine, politics, evangelization, and much more. It also raises anew the question of loyalties—Is one first and foremost a part of the worldwide body of Christ, for whom baptism marks entry into the new community gathered and sealed by the risen Lord, or is one primarily a citizen of one or another nation, empire, or state? My colleague Peggy Levitt at Wellesley University writes on Christian migrants from the Dominican Republic, who show up in Massachusetts with a letter of introduction from the pastor back home— an example of the baptismal certificate being more important than the passport.

Things like this serve as a vivid reminder that when it's self-aware, the Church is larger than any nation, more diverse than any region, more deeply rooted in the life of the poor than any other entity that would claim us. In a global perspective, it's the Church that is truly the polity that makes one out of many (*e pluribus unum*, and all that); states, countries, ethnicities, tribes, and classes look like sectarian enclaves in comparison.

Imagine the possibilities if issues like immigration inspire the Church to take its more transnational nature more seriously—think of the things that might change, that might be reconsidered. It may well be the stranger, the foreigner, and the poor in our midst who help the Church learn in our time and place what it means to "seek first the Kingdom of God."

CHAPTER 6

Mapping the Maps:
A Christian Guide to Christian Guides to Politics[1]

INTRODUCTION

Earlier this year, as part of my Lenten discipline (never very strong even in good years), I took it upon myself to read material I generally tried to avoid, all of which by coincidence seemed to deal with Christianity and the electoral process.

I'm not sure how it worked as a devotional practice, nor whether it helped me bond more deeply with the passion of Jesus, but it did give me a chance to compare perspectives and voices not usually looked at side by side. It was an exercise that was simultaneously enlightening, depressing, and even chilling, at least when viewed from a regard for the integrity of the gospel in our time and place.

As the primary season turned into the general election—with both parties' nominees sitting down for a heartfelt chat with none other than Rick Warren while on national television—it's interesting to see how Christianity is in play in this presidential election. Everyone seems interested in constructing, cajoling, and channeling the Christian vote—if there is such a thing—in one direction or another, resulting in a plethora of guidebooks to how followers of Jesus should think about the political system. It's my pleasure to join you this evening to reflect on these

1. Delivered to the Wesley Center at Oklahoma State University, October 27, 2008.

reflections, to provide something of a guide to the guidebooks, for lack of a better phrase; in so doing, I hope to push a bit beyond the specifics of the respective agendas to focus on some of the deeper and—at least from the perspective of the church's long-term mission—more important assumptions about discipleship, being part of the body of Christ, and matters of allegiance and loyalty.

The material I'll review with you tonight are as follows:

- *The Great Awakening: Reviving Faith and Politics in a Post-Religious Right America*, by Jim Wallis;

- *How Would Jesus Vote? A Christian Perspective on the Issues*, by D. James Kennedy (with Jerry Newcombe); and

- *Forming Consciences For Faithful Citizenship*, by the United States Conference of Catholic Bishops.

In addition (as if this isn't enough for us), it's probably important to revisit the tempest over Reverend Jeremiah Wright and the Obama campaign, since this illustrates some additional concerns on matters of the sacred and the nature of mainstream politics. So, in order to discern the heart of the gospel in the midst of a presidential campaign, with so many voices clamoring for our allegiance and commitment, let's try to make some sense of some of the themes, assertions, and visions on offer all around us.

WALLIS AND KENNEDY: POLAR OPPOSITES OR A BALANCED TICKET?

It's probably safe to assume that Jim Wallis and D. James Kennedy are a fairly unlikely couple, While they acknowledge one another as fellow Christians, they probably situate one another as far apart as possible while inhabiting the same country. Kennedy, as some of you may know, until his death last year was pastor of Coral Ridge Presbyterian Church in Florida, a conservative megachurch with an extensive broadcasting ministry and leadership role in the evangelical political movement of the past few decades. Wallis, for his part, is an evangelical pastor and leader of the Sojourners community based in Washington DC; he edits the magazine of the same name, is a bestselling author, and a longtime advocate for Christian involvement in progressive social and political causes.

In many ways, each pastor speaks to and for very different constituencies and agendas. Wallis's *The Great Awakening* suggests that large and important change is just around the corner, if only Christians recognize and seize the moment. "Something is happening. Faith is being applied to social justice in ways that we might have never imagined just a few short years ago."[2] More specifically, "I believe we are poised on the edge of what might become another spiritual revival or awakening that will change things—big things in the world. We may be seeing the beginning of a revival for justice" (6–7).

"Awakening" is a key category throughout Jim Wallis's life—I have been reading him for more than thirty years (I can even remember that *Sojourners* was originally known as the "Post-American," a community and journal opposed to American imperialism and its domestication of the Church), and I've lost track of how many times Jim Wallis has predicted or perceived a new awakening just around the corner, just about to arrive. His most recent guide to Christian political engagement proceeds by seeking "not simply to address the issues, but rather to identify the values that are necessary for social change. Our values lead to commitments. With each commitment, the application of energy and constituencies of faith could provide what is needed for real change" (8). In each chapter, he aims to "demonstrate the theological foundations and the moral principles that undergird the political goals we seek." Such will be grounded in biblical materials for "people of the book," or in the "most moral values" of others (8)—an important methodological step, one that requires "teaching religious people how to make their appeals in moral language and secular people not to fear that such appeals will lead to theocracy" (27).

Kennedy, for his part, echoes Wallis when he writes that "Clearly, our country is in a great need of a true awakening. I believe it is our only real hope."[3] When looking at what he considers the sad state of affairs in American life—secular humanism, abortion, same-sex marriage, insufficient patriotism, and more—Kennedy concludes that "a great deal of the

2. Wallis, *Great Awakening*, 1. Further references will be given parenthetically in the text.

3. Kennedy, *How Would Jesus Vote?*, 1. Further references will be given parenthetically in the text.

blame for the state of the nation must fall on *us*. It must be placed at the doorstep of the church" (8).

Where Wallis's method involves translating biblical imperatives and norms into language accessible to non-believers (Wallis believes such can be done without distorting or diluting them in the process), Kennedy's book makes a methodological move that, ironically enough, seems to subvert his title question of "How Would Jesus Vote?" As Kennedy writes, "Some may quibble that we should look only at what Jesus said as opposed to the whole Bible. Yet Jesus put His seal of approval on the Old Testament as the Word of God . . ." Kennedy adds that "Jesus commissioned the writing of the New Testament to record his words and the further revelation He would give through the Holy Spirit" (11–12).

All of which means, in other words, "When we ask 'How would Jesus have us vote?' we are actually asking 'How would the Bible have us vote?'" (12). Thanks to this move, we get relatively little Jesus in *How Would Jesus Vote?* Instead, we get a great deal of the Old Testament and the usual passages from Paul on civil authority—important matters, to be sure, but an approach that avoids the most politically subversive aspects of Jesus as presented in the Sermon on the Mount, for example.

For the late Reverend Kennedy, the Christian role in American life is that of a beleaguered minority, despite the fact that the overwhelming majority of Americans claim to be Christians. To Kennedy, "The problem is that, although there are many Christians in this country, though we can say that 36 percent of adults claim they have had a conversion experience, and though that number is growing, it is still a minority . . . Though Christianity is a growing force in this country, it is still far from being the controlling force."

Wallis and Kennedy, then, seem to occupy two very different positions in the American political and religious landscape. But when read together, one sees some very strong commonalities, shared assumptions that I suggest are more important than the different policy choices each advocates. Each sees Christian faith as but the fuel for the real business of our day, namely national politics. Each uses the Bible as a policy manual, deriving political imperatives for state action that carry the legitimacy of scriptural warrant. And each, in his own way, seems to sacralize the polity, making the national community and not the Church the true bearer of God's witness, presence, and action in the world. Let me explore these commonalities in a bit more detail.

Faith as Fuel

Since he writes less about the nuts-and-bolts of electoral politics than does Wallis, Kennedy's advocacy of faith as the fuel for political action occurs less often. Still, it appears regularly in *How Would Jesus Vote?*, and is assumed throughout. The Church must engage in political action to clean up the mess that is American politics; being a Christian is supposed to move persons beyond indecision and into action (188); and Christians active in politics "can actually make a difference as to how much of our world is occupied by Christ versus how much is occupied by the devil" (18).

Faith-as-fuel is a major theme in Wallis's book—indeed, the entire book may be read as a brief for how Christian faith can sustain people's commitment to the work of secular politics. Religion may, according to Wallis, be "the catalyst that could provide the tipping point in finding solutions to the biggest and most significant moral and social causes of our world today." He adds that "we have some real mountains to move in our world today—problems and challenges so big that they become a job for faith, a job for spiritual power applied to social change" (3). Personal and social conversion go hand in hand in Wallis's view of how Christians can serve the political order: "Faith can provide the fire, the passion, the strength, the perseverance, and the hope necessary for social movements to win, and to change politics" (21).

The Bible as Policy Manual

If the job of Christianity is to provide energy for persons joining the political campaigns of Obama and McCain, they are sent there with very different lists of agenda items to pursue, according to Kennedy and Wallis. For Kennedy, voting as Jesus would vote (remember, Jesus doesn't really get much of a say in *How Would Jesus Vote?*) means seeing to it that the state adopt the proper biblical positions on the following issues: the life issues (abortion, stem cells, suicide, and euthanasia), but also capital punishment, war, Islamic terrorism, electoral reform, religion in schools, social security, tax policy, trade policy, support for capitalism, private property, the welfare state, health care, climate change, ecology, poverty, immigration, assimilation and civic formation, citizenship, marriage and family, feminism and homosexuality, pornography, judicial activism, federal judicial appointments, and divorce (I stopped keeping count after a while).

For Wallis, the biblical imperatives for state action include the life issues, but also political corruption, the environment, family and gay rights, war, poverty, economic inequality, race, international debt and development, climate change, cultural diversity, immigration, feminism, Darfur, the United Nations, torture, capital punishment, terrorism and policing (I lost track here too). Both pastors make a fairly unconvincing bow to non-partisanship, which does little to erase the recognition that their guidance puts Christians at odds with one another in pursuit of political goals—the unity of the Church is a casualty of the need to seize state power, inasmuch as the state now seems to be the arena in which God now acts most determinatively.

Sacralizing the Body Politic

Both Kennedy and Wallis deny that their guidebooks replace the Church with the state, that they confer upon the political body the sort of devotion and allegiance rightly claimed only by the church as God's body in the world. Upon inspection, however, both seem to do so—their use of Romans 13 is similarly uncritical and decontextualized in important ways, for example, leading to different paths toward the sacralizing of America. Kennedy's use of Matt 22:15–22 ("Give to Caesar what is Caesar's . . ."), for example, is so broad as to make state-defined norms of "good citizenship" a religious duty overriding all other claims. "It is our duty [on biblical grounds]," writes Kennedy, "to do what good citizenship requires" (25). Among other things, this means that "it is a sin *not* to vote . . . [aside from rare occasions] if you do not render to Caesar your obligation as a citizen of this country, my friend, it is a sin" (32).

Wallis, for his part, stops short of turning the right to vote into a Christian obligation, owed as a matter of obedience to Christ. Wallis makes sacred the national community in another way, making "America" the bearer of divine promise and hopes in language more properly used for the Church. "I want people to dream big dreams, to tell America it is okay to have ideals and work toward cultural and political transformation" (9). Throughout *The Great Awakening*, Wallis's use of collective pronouns reveals that to him the real agent of awakening in the world is not God's Church, but America. "America is eager," "America is ready," "America has dreams"—not the Church. The sacralizing of the collective person "America" also involves, albeit casually, the subordination of the Church. At one point Wallis quotes Martin Luther King Jr., writing that "The church must be reminded that it is not the master or the servant of the state, but rather the conscience of the state." Such a quote could stand as a perfect definition of chaplaincy, of the reduction of the Church's cosmic role in God's plan to assuaging the consciences of the powerful; the Jesuits of old would have endorsed this view, even as they whispered in the ears of princes and rulers of the world.

FAITHFUL CITIZENSHIP

If Wallis and Kennedy move toward sacralizing the polity at the expense of the Church, such sacralizing is even more apparent in *Faithful Citizenship*, the most recent guide to politics and faith issued by the Catholic Bishops of the United States.[4] While faith-and-politics statements have long been issued by bureaucrats speaking on behalf of the bishops, *Faithful Citizenship* stands out as the only one voted on and endorsed by the entirety of the Catholic hierarchy in the United States. In many ways it is an interesting document, one that nonetheless shares many of the same shortcomings apparent in Kennedy's and Wallis's guides to the faithful.

Much more so than Wallis and Kennedy, the bishops seem to collapse the distinction between citizen and Christian. In the first two pages of this guide, the bishops repeatedly blur to the point of erasure the distinction between being an American and being a Christian. "We the nation," "we as society, we as country" are the categories of address, not "we the Church" or "we the followers of Christ."

Central to the aims of this document is the notion of "formation"— that is, the process by which people come to internalize the affections, dispositions, priorities, and commitments of Jesus. Disciples are made, not born, and a Christ-filled conscience is simultaneously a gift from God and the result of faithful learning, reflection, and mentoring by elders in the faith. These sorts of considerations are implied but underdeveloped in other works, including those of Wallis and Kennedy, and processes of

4. References to the work will also be given parenthetically in the text.

Christian formation have become a central concern for all churches—Protestant, Catholic, and Orthodox—in contemporary times.

In *Faithful Citizenship*, the general idea is that it is the Church's responsibility to help form conscience, and the moral responsibility of individual Catholic Christians is "to hear, receive, and act upon the Church's moral teaching in the lifelong task of forming his or her own conscience. With this foundation, Catholics are better able to evaluate policy positions, party platforms, and candidates' promises and actions in light of the Gospel and the moral and social teaching of the church in order to help build a better world." This raises some questions we will return to later, but the basic assumption is that the Church helps individuals form consciences, which presumably will correspond in some significant sense to what the Church teaches in social and political life (e.g., respect for life, concern for the common good, peace as a social priority).

Lest any of this smack of authoritarianism or a Catholic cabal of the sort so well exploited by anti-Catholic movements in U.S. history, the bishops assert that "we bishops do not intend to tell Catholics for whom or against whom to vote . . . We recognize that the responsibility to make moral choices in political life rests with each individual in light of a properly formed conscience" (par. 7).

Like Wallis and Kennedy, the bishops sacralize political participation, claiming that "participation in political life is a moral obligation" (par. 13). The obligation to participate in political life, according to the bishops, is supposed to produce something other than traditional interest-group politics and a clash of powerful special interests; it is a well-formed conscience that is intended to give rise to "the dignity of every human being, the pursuit of the common good, and the protection of the weak and vulnerable" (par. 14).

But what is conscience, and how does one know whether it is "well-formed"? According to *Faithful Citizenship*:

> Conscience is not something that allows us to justify doing whatever we want, nor is it a mere "feeling" about what we should or should not do. Rather, conscience is the voice of God resounding in the human heart, revealing the truth to us and calling us to do what is good while shunning what is evil. Conscience always requires serious attempts to make sound moral judgments based on the truths of our faith. (par. 17)

The formation of conscience includes several elements. First, there is the desire to embrace goodness and truth. For Catholics this begins with a willingness and openness to seek the truth and what is right by studying Sacred Scripture and the teaching of the Church as contained in the Catechism of the Catholic Church. It is also important to examine the facts and background information about various choices. Finally, prayerful reflection is essential to discern the will of God. Catholics must also understand that if they fail to form their consciences they can make erroneous judgments. (par. 18)

Essential in all of this is the role of prudence, a virtue that when cultivated and practiced produces some ability to see how to do good and avoid evil in particular situations. Not all situations are clear-cut, not every choice is such that one can easily do the good. There do exist, however, those things the Christian tradition has long referred to as "intrinsically evil" deeds—things that are always wrong to do, regardless of situation or context. The bishops are worth quoting on this point:

There are some things we must never do, as individuals or as a society, because they are always incompatible with love of God and neighbor. Such actions are so deeply flawed that they are always opposed to the authentic good of persons. These are called "intrinsically evil" actions. They must always be rejected and opposed and must never be supported or condoned. A prime example is the intentional taking of innocent human life, as in abortion and euthanasia . . . Other direct assaults on innocent human life and violations of human dignity, such as genocide, torture, racism, and the targeting of noncombatants in acts of terror or war, can never be justified. (pars. 22–23).

Here's where things start to get challenging. The document favorably quotes a Vatican document that observes that "a well-formed Christian conscience does not permit one to vote for a political program or an individual law which contradicts the fundamental contents of faith and morals." Presumably, they refer here to abortion and euthanasia, among other things. But, at the same time, the bishops note two problems they want to avoid: a sort of flattening of issues that makes these "intrinsic evils" just one issue among others (abortion is as important as gun control or campaign finance, for example); and on the other hand, a elevation of intrinsically evil issues like abortion over everything else, such that one can ignore a candidate's views on war, racism, the environment, and so on.

So here's the box the bishops have painted themselves into with this guide: some issues are of fundamental importance, but the bishops are opposed to single-issue voting. But what to do when confronted with what—after thirty-five years—seems to be a structural, not merely contingent, feature of American politics: one party ideologically committed to abortion on demand but occasionally less bad on other things, with the other party pragmatically opposed to abortion but deficient on most of the other issues defined as essential to the common good?

Well, one could just refuse to dignify such a structure by withholding participation and the allegiance it implies—refusing to participate in a systematic neglect of the common good and the human community. In fact, as we shall see, increasing numbers of Christians are starting to see a principled refusal to dignify such a system as something consistent with, and perhaps logically entailed by, a notion of Christian discipleship that sees killing as incompatible with following a crucified Lord who disarmed his followers and counseled love of enemies.

The bishops, like Kennedy and Wallis, recoil from the suggestion that voting might be incompatible with discipleship, calling its refusal an "extraordinary step" of a generally undesirable sort. Instead, the bishops suggest that someone "may decide to vote for the candidate deemed less likely to advance such a morally flawed position and more likely to pursue other authentic human goods." While presumably the counsel here is about abortion—go ahead and vote for someone opposed to church teaching so long as he or she is doing something worthwhile on other issues—one wonders how such counsel would sound if the issue in question is something else, like rape, random executions, or eliminating racial minorities (other intrinsically evil acts according to church teaching). One finds it difficult to imagine Christians pledging allegiance to a system routinely practicing such—being a Christian might logically entail resistance or non-cooperation with such a structure rather than directives to participate as part of one's sacred duty.

So what? In *Faithful Citizenship* (as with the guides produced by Wallis and Kennedy), there is no mention of the Church's abysmal failure to form consciences in harmony with the gospel. The inability of churches across confessional divides to form people into more than nominal or cultural Christians is one of the scandals of our age, with the Catholics leading the way as the least effective in forming the affections, dispositions, and priorities of its would-be adherents (mainline Protestants are almost as bad, and evangelical churches exhibit a range of other pathologies in practices of congregational formation).

As a result, one gets a poorly articulated relationship between "conscience" as an individual matter and "Christian conscience" as a communal product and process. The lack of any sort of Church discipline—calling to account the laity, clergy, politicians or anyone else—means that church leaders like the U.S. bishops offer pious platitudes that pull in opposite directions all the time, not just occasionally. But because they can't imagine a "plague on all their houses" sort of position, for example, or a refusal to legitimate systems that routinely force people to choose which set of intrinsic evils they will support, the bishops are left to equivocate and evade the implications of their own lack of political and ecclesial analysis.

What is missing in all these guides, however much they differ among themselves, is a robust sense of Church—what difference it might mean that Christians are not merely (nor primarily) citizens, but by virtue of baptism are made part of a new people, made distinct from the peoples of the world to continue with the help of the Holy Spirit the work of Jesus of Nazareth as reflected in the gospels. Christians follow a most unusual sort of king, one who disarmed his followers and made them part of a body wider and larger than any nation, more pluralistic than any state, and committed to the audacious notion that a community can be constituted by forgiveness and mutuality instead of by force and violence.

No review of guidelines for Christians in politics would be complete, during this unusual electoral season, without revisiting the drama of Obama and Reverend Jeremiah Wright. If Wallis, Kennedy, and the U.S. Catholic bishops explore varieties of politics-as-liturgy, events involving Wright serve to identify borders, limits, and the realm of sacrilege. While not found in a single volume, one can find the "text" of the Wright guidebook in the way I did—reading interview transcripts, a series of major speeches, press conferences, sermons in their entirety, and the near-limitless output of commentators.

As a brief recap, you'll recall that the GOP and the Clinton campaign both drew attention to a pair of Wright sermons (short clips of which were posted on YouTube), involving the phrase "God damn America," and "chickens coming home to roost." Wright was vilified as a venomous preacher of hatred and anti-Americanism, enabling Clinton and the

Republicans to attack Obama for having such an ideologue as a mentor and spiritual leader.

Not surprisingly, the snippets of Wright's sermon were bereft of context in order to provoke maximal outrage. The "God Damn America" sermon, which was actually entitled "Confusing God and Government," was delivered on April 23, 2003. In it, Wright notes that all governments lie while claiming to tell the truth, and that all governments—the Roman Empire, the British, the Japanese, the Germans—fail, and fail to do justice to its citizens. He then lists several instances in which the United States has failed its citizens—its Native Americans, its citizens of African descent, its citizens of Japanese descent during the Second World War—and even as its failures continue into the current era, the United States invokes the blessings of God upon itself. No, says Wright, not blessings but curses come from a just God—"Not God Bless America but God Damn America! That's in the Bible. For killing innocent people. God Damn America for treating us citizens as less than human. God Damn America as long as she tries to act like she is God and she is Supreme." Strong stuff, to be sure, but hardly a frothing example of national hatred.

The second incendiary clip came from Wright's post-September 11, 2001, sermon, wherein he said that with the attacks, "America's chickens were coming home to roost." The Clinton and Republican campaigns seized upon the phrase as proof of Wright's hatred of America, suggesting that the United States deserved the attacks or did something to bring them on. Such is a heresy across the board in the church of America, and woe to anyone who suggests that the United States might not be innocent and virtuous in the world.

In fact, the "chickens coming home to roost" line was not original to Wright, but was used more than forty years before by Malcolm X—who was vilified for it. In the Wright sermon, ironically enough, the pastor was paraphrasing its use by a white U.S. ambassador after the September 11 attacks.

No matter—Wright was seen as toxic to the Obama campaign, a voice so far beyond the realm of acceptable discourse that he had to be "managed." The Obama campaign adopted several tactics in attempts to do so:

1. Patronizing: Obama described Wright as being old, cranky, from another generation, and limited by his experience of segregation—in effect, Obama adopted the posture of "I don't agree with him, but you have

to understand the limits of his world." Obama compared him to his maternal grandmother, from whom impolitic and racially insensitive comments would flow on occasion—you can't dump your family no matter how they might embarrass themselves.

2. Distancing: When a smiling shake of the head didn't dislodge the controversy, Obama moved quickly to distinguish his fondness for Trinity United Church of Christ—its social programs, its leadership role in the community—from the preaching of Wright, whose anti-Americanism he disliked and disregarded.

3. Excommunication: the last step in the process, in which Obama vigorously repudiated Wright and his preaching.

This last step, one Obama's campaign hoped to avoid, became "necessary" after the controversy around Wright refused to fade after a few weeks. Most upsetting to Obama's people was that Wright dared to defend himself against the calumny heaped upon him—the nerve of him, answering his critics. Didn't he realize that the most important goal for all of black America, indeed for all of America, is to elect Obama as president? How dare he interfere.

The final Obama denunciation—expulsion from the Church of "Change You Can Believe In"—came in the following remarks:

> When he equates the United States wartime efforts with terrorism, then there are no excuses. They offend me. They rightly offend all Americans. And they should be denounced.

Further, Obama states:

> I don't think he showed much concern for what we are trying to do in this campaign and what we're trying to do for the American people.[5]

But what did Wright say in describing his view of God and the church? Here's a sample from his National Press Club remarks:

> The prophetic theology of the black church is not only a theology of liberation; it is also a theology of transformation, which is also rooted in Isaiah 61, the text from which Jesus preached in his inaugural message . . .

5. Obama, "Remarks on Wright."

God's desire is for positive, meaningful, and permanent change. God does not want one people seeing themselves as superior to other people. God does not want the powerless masses, the poor, the widows, the marginalized, and those underserved by the powerful few to stay locked into sick systems which treat some in the society as being more equal than others in that society.[6]

It is significant, I think, that in responding to Wright's press conference and speech to the NAACP, Obama made the following statement:

You know, when I go to church, it's not for spectacle. It's to pray and to find—to find a stronger sense of faith. It's not to posture politically. It's not—you know, it's not to hear things that violate my core beliefs.[7]

In that one line—"it's not to hear things that violate my core beliefs"—beliefs about America, more specifically—Obama serves notice that no prophets need apply, that his is an altogether bourgeois and American notion of a God that cheerleads and encourages and comforts us in what we've already decided to do. Faith is fuel for Obama, as it is for Wallis and Kennedy and the Catholic bishops, and nothing more than that. Had Wright stayed within the bounds of a powerbroker preacher impressed with himself, he would have been nothing more than a bit player in the drama; but to the extent that something of the radical gospel actually intruded, the Obama machine wasted no time in casting him into the darkness, the space reserved for conspiracy theorists, cranks, and lunatics (Wright even complained that his critics made him out to be a "whack-a-doodle").

Double-standards and ironies abound here on many levels, to be sure. When no less a character than Frankie Schaeffer—son of Francis and Edith Schaeffer, among the intellectual progenitors of the religious right in the 1970s and 1980s—becomes a voice of perspective, you know you are in unusual times. The younger Schaeffer, who served as his father's aide and loyal follower before converting to the Orthodox Church, noted that his father frequently described the United States as cursed by God, as perhaps the Whore of Babylon for its embrace of legal abortion and infanticide—and was rewarded with an invitation to the White House under Ronald Reagan, and cheered by the religious right. When the black pastor

6. Wright, "African-American Religious Experience."
7. Obama, "Remarks on Wright."

Wright makes less incendiary comparisons, by contrast, he becomes a heretic and a traitor, one beyond the pale of acceptable worship. As if to prove his bona fides in the worship of America, Wright trotted out his record of military service and all the young people his church sends into the armed forces; his prophetic witness itself being policed by patriotism, albeit with different calibrations than those employed by Obama and his followers.

We don't have time to look at them in any detail, but before the election I'd encourage you to consult either of these two Christian voting guides: *Jesus for President*, by Shane Claiborne and Chris Haw, and *Electing Not to Vote*, edited by Ted Lewis. Let me give you just a taste from both, and you'll see how they compare to the guides we've already mentioned, and in fact how they dramatize the deep similarities despite surface differences among Wallis, Kennedy, and the U.S. Catholic bishops.

One of the things that makes these guides different is a different sort of diagnosis or assessment of the problem of Christians and politics. According to Claiborne and Haw:

> We are seeing more and more that the church has fallen in love with the state and that this love affair is killing the church's imagination. The powerful benefits and temptations of running the world's largest superpower have bent the church's identity. Having power at its fingertips, the church often finds "guiding the course of history" a more alluring goal than following the crucified Christ. Too often the patriotic values of pride and strength triumph over the spiritual values of humility, gentleness, and sacrificial love.[8]

Jesus for President is a popular and pretty book that popularizes much of what others have been teaching for some time. The book offers a walk through the Scriptures, identifying the peculiarity of Israel's political vision (and how the Israelites fell short), and of the New Testament's treatment of Jesus and his politics, the nature of the Church, and concepts like power, citizenship, allegiance, kingdom, wealth, and sacrifice. Its chapter titles include "When the Empire Got Baptized," "A Peculiar Party" (referring to the Church, not the Democrats), and several other things not likely to be found in the other sort of guides.

---

8. Claiborne and Haw, *Jesus for President*, 17.

For his part, Lewis notes that voting is far more than a simple, dispassionate practice.

> Voting for political leaders, whether we think about it or not, establishes bonds between people and governments in similar ways that religion establishes bonds between peoples and deities . . . [S]uch bonds of allegiance do not fit within the new vision of community set forth in the New Testament. On the positive side, this new vision suggests that our choosing, binding, promising, pledging, and vowing energies are to be expressed for the sake of the ekklesia, the "called-out" community, and are not to be expressed for the upbuilding of a state, nation, or empire.[9]

Neither Claiborne nor Lewis and his contributors have a single position on voting, other than to be skeptical of the claim that voting is a "sacred duty" or an obligatory way for the church to live as followers of the risen Lord. For Claiborne,

> The distinctly kingdom question is not about how we should vote but about how we should live. The decision we make in each future election is no more important than how we vote every day. We vote every day for companies, for people, and we put money toward "campaigns." We need to think of the faces behind the scenes. Who are the masters and Caesars that we pledge allegiance to by the way we live and through the things we put our trust in? We vote every day with our feet, our hands, our lips, and our wallets.[10]

Do Claiborne and the contributors to the Lewis volume dictate only one properly Christian response to the matter of mainstream politics? No. Claiborne encourages people to consider subversive ways of thinking about voting: for example, instead of using it as an exercise in self-interest (what policies will be best for me, what does my "autonomous self" prefer?), he offers stories and possibilities of several sorts—including that of a community whose members engage in reflection with immigrants and undocumented persons, and vote the way those folks think is best. Lewis's book, for its part, showcases scholars and church leaders with a variety of perspectives—refusing to vote in a particular election (because both candidates are too far afield from a minimal Christian disposition on key

9. Lewis, *Electing Not to Vote*, 101.

10. Claiborn and Haw, *Jesus for* President, 334.

questions), or refusing to vote for some offices (abstaining from national elections but voting in local ones), or refusing to vote altogether (from a conviction that voting represents a pledge of allegiance to something other than the God of Jesus Christ, or from a consistent sort of Christian pacifism that refuses to participate in the lethality that is politics as practiced by national states). Both books are worth your time, both deserve serious consideration, and either of them stands as a challenging alternative to the directives issued by the likes of Wallis, Kennedy, and the Catholic bishops.

CHAPTER 7

Race to Divide:
The Limits and Hopes of Ecclesial Formation[1]

If you've been to a gathering of the Ekklesia Project before, you know
that a common phrase to explain much of what we're about refers to the
church as our "first family," in terms of shaping and ordering our desires,
affections, and practices. In bringing together some of what we've been
talking about this week, about how the church as our first family ought to
engage questions of race and racism, it's probably essential to talk briefly
about the biological family and how it forms and deforms things as well.
In my own case, it's a matter of family stories told and untold.

I grew up in the blue-collar town of Joliet, Illinois. My family in
many ways was the poster child for blue-collar populism: tenant farmers
(sounds so much better than the southern term "sharecropper," but it was
the same thing) on one side, coal miners, truck drivers, and Teamsters
organizers on the other.

I used to think there were only two kinds of religion in my home
town, based on the school system—there were Catholics and publics.
Only later in this strongly blue-collar, Catholic town did it dawn on me

1. A Plenary Address to "Crossing the Racial Divide: Race, Racism and the Body of
Christ," Annual Gathering of The Ekklesia Project, July 10, 2008.

that there were so many different varieties of you Protestants—like so many exotic birds or tropical fish. Just keeping all the names straight and recognizing the identifying plumage was great fun and a fine way to while away one's free time.

In many ways it was a Catholic ghetto, with all varieties of Catholics, except for black Catholics. We didn't know there were any. In fact, growing up, I cannot remember one sermon on race preached in any Catholic church I encountered during my first eighteen years of life.

When it came to matters of race, my family demonstrated what may have been a fairly typical sort of schizophrenia of the time. From them, I learned of Jesus and a Christian life, doing the right thing even if unpopular, concern for the disadvantaged, and public service as a virtuous thing. But race and black people were the exception to much of that.

My father had a few black friends in the military, and a white life before and after. He was something of a reluctant warrior in the civil rights movement—as a federal employee, he was sent south as a poll watcher and election observer, sent to Selma and Mississippi, and had run-ins with white supremacists like Byron de la Beckwith and his followers. But my father didn't want to be there, and he especially didn't like agitators; the strong dislike of agitators no matter what the issue led him to vote for segregationist governor of Alabama, George Wallace, in his independent bid for the president. My father was the only man I ever met who voted for George Wallace . . . twice. When Martin Luther King Jr. was assassinated and riots erupted in my home town, the city fathers' response was to raise the bridges across the river that separated the black and white sections of town. My father's response was to buy a new box of double-ought buck shotgun shells just in case. He did move forward on matters of race over the years, but like for many people, the starting point seemed several steps toward the back.

I loved my father, although ours was a complicated relationship, but I adored my grandfather—even though he only had an eighth-grade education, he was what I thought a man should be. My grandfather, however, is a case study in why privileging "personal experience" is a bad method for theological ethics. His encounters with minorities—blacks as strikebreakers and scabs while he tried to organize in the labor movement beginning in the 1930s, and a special dislike of Mexicans courtesy of one particularly vicious mugging in which he was cut up rather seriously while fighting off several at one time—left him with a degree of racial animosity that was as unpolished as it was unapologetic. For what it was worth, he also used to refer jokingly—I think he was joking, but one was never too sure—to his well-defined hierarchy of undesirability from which no ethnic group was excluded: Poles, Hungarians, Italians, Greeks, English. He seemed especially fond of disparaging my grandmother's Irish heritage even while he displayed a few of the less flattering traits embodied in the Irish stereotype.

In my family's circle, the wonder of a black friend among my parents and their contemporaries was always something of note—as rare as a red calf or a winning lottery ticket, but worthy of much discussion when such did present itself. These friends, however few in number, were almost always made at work, given that their church and neighborhood were all white when I was a kid—and the praises showered upon such exotic friends often seemed to emphasize all the ways in which these friends were like stereotypical white people.

It was Thanksgiving of 1976. I had just started college a few weeks before, the first in my family privileged enough to leave home to do so— my first time on my own, my first extended stretch away from home. My mother made a generous offer during those early weeks, encouraging me to invite to our house for Thanksgiving whomever of my new friends couldn't afford to return home for the holiday. I gladly took her up on her offer and extended an invitation, but when she eventually realized that my new friend from Birmingham, Alabama, was black, the conversation went dead. You will have to withdraw the invitation, she said, because my father will not sit down to eat with a black person. I will not keep my father away from the dinner table because of your friend, she continued, so you'll have to tell your friend that there has been a change in plans. I offered my friend a transparent excuse for having to withdraw the invitation, but the effect was immediate—a new friendship shattered beyond repair, leaving me buried under shame, guilt, powerlessness, and an eventual determination that I would never be put in that position again, and would cease being governed by racial rules I neither made nor endorsed. In part this moment of deep shame pushed me to stretch myself, widen my world, enter new neighborhoods, new lives, and new stories. I have no illusions about having been "cured" of racism—my past and white America's racial thinking will always be a part of me—but I desired to do better, or at least to make more interesting mistakes in trying to purge the evil from my life.

Why I'm Here Today

Since 1996, my family and I have been part of a predominantly African-American Catholic congregation. It's a small congregation, probably no more than two hundred families on the membership roll, and probably 75 percent black, most of the rest being white folks with a few Latinos, and a visiting African or Asian-American from time to time. My children were the "diversity" in the children's choir when they joined, our church's worship style is black gospel music, and people sometimes get excited about the Lord, and with the exception of our pastor almost all of the leadership positions and all of the staff positions are held by African-Americans.

African-American Catholicism is an unusual force in the American ecclesial world—a double-minority (Catholicism as a minority in the black community, blacks as a minority in Catholic America) that has confronted suspicion and rejection from both sides for hundreds of years. Not merely surviving, African-American Catholicism has become a movement with well over 2 million members—were they their own denomination, they would be the second or third largest African-American church tradition in the United States; instead, they represent fewer than 5 percent of Catholics in the United States, with regional strengths in cities like Chicago and New York, and in states including Louisiana.

Of all the various combinations of groups that could make a church "multiracial" according to the definitions used (and mentioned previously) by sociologists like Michael Emerson and Christian Smith, my church represents the most difficult sort of combination. It's easier to create and sustain a multiracial church that is, for example, white and Latino or white and Asian, or black and Latino, or black and Asian, than it is to create and sustain a congregation that mixes blacks and whites. One of the reasons this is so, according to Emerson, is that for historical reasons black and white cultures are the two "indigenous American cultures" to which all newcomers have to relate, adjust, or learn to navigate. Two-thirds of all multiracial congregations in the U.S. are something other than black-and-white, and black-white congregations have the most severe internal conflicts.[2]

Such conflict, says Emerson, reflects that "people of both indigenous U.S. cultures believe they have, at the very least, an equal right to practice their culture; have little interest in giving it up; have oppositional cultures,

2. Emerson, *People of the Dream*, 134–35, 139.

so that adopting one may be seen as denying the other; have cultures that have been institutionalized through, among other things, separate denominations and congregations; and have centuries of racial wounds." Emerson reports that multiracial congregations generally only appeal to one or the other of these two indigenous cultures, that is, a Black-Latino congregation is less likely to draw whites, while a white-Latino congregation will tend to be less interesting to blacks.[3]

For reasons like these, apparently, congregations like mine are unusual on a variety of levels. We're an oddity within the Catholic world, we're an oddity within the black and white communities, and we've been an intentionally African-American parish for several decades. It hasn't always been this way, of course. It so happens that this parish is the one in which my parents and grandparents were both married, where blacks and Latinos were made to feel unwelcome for decades (for that matter, it was an Italian parish in which my Irish ancestors were made to feel unwelcome) by a pastor who used the pulpit on a regular basis to denounce Franklin Roosevelt as a dangerous socialist.

I suppose the reason that I'm here rather than other members of my congregation is that the sort of questions that animate the Ekklesia Project—wanting a more radical notion of church, getting beyond what we sometimes call the Constantinian notion of public policy and the government as the central focus of Christian social witness—are most definitely not very interesting to most members of my church, from the pastor on down. Drawing deeply from the history of the black church and working-class Catholicism, my church in many ways considers community organizing, pressuring elected officials, and helping elect sympathetic figures as the eighth sacrament in Catholic life and practice. In the eyes of my church, Saul Alinsky, considered by many to be the father of modern community organizing, was present at the Last Supper, the thirteenth apostle behind the scenes organizing the waiters and waitresses for a future demonstration and workplace shutdown.

As a result, much of what we talk about in and through the Ekklesia Project strikes them as less than compelling—interesting, good points made, but not the sort of thing that might make anyone shift emphasis from a voter-registration drive to something else. And so, like many of you here today, I live in some tension with my own congregation—wanting

3. Ibid., 139, 141.

the church to build a common life, to demand more from us than voting for the Democratic Party and filling buses to go bother state legislators in Springfield on a regular basis. I want more, and I get less—and like many of you, I have to figure out what to do with that.

Still, while my particular take on the church and the world isn't widely shared, my church allows me to use whatever it is I'm good at for the benefit of the church. I've taught Scripture study classes that smuggled in the sort of reading of the gospel of Mark, for example, that has upended so many of us here thanks to people like Ched Meyers and Daniel Berrigan. In recent years, I've found occasions to introduce to my congregation some of the troublemakers that inhabit the Ekklesia Project orbit—many of you know Emmanuel Katongole, who splits his time at Duke University (where he runs a church-focused Center on Reconciliation) and his duties as a parish priest in Uganda. Thanks to having brought my church and my friend Emmanuel together, our small congregation decided that we'd go into the drinking water business; with usually fewer than a hundred people attending on Sunday morning, our church has managed to raise and donate money for five clean-water wells in Uganda in only three years. None of which involved the government, or a political campaign, or legislative action—just connecting one part of the worldwide body of Christ with another, and having the common water of baptism be the shared symbol that tied life in one place to enabling life in another. That ours is a black church involved with other black churches takes away some of the potential ambiguity in partnering with churches and people in Africa; more than once I have heard African-American colleagues wonder why some white churches find enthusiasm for work with African churches—which are exotic, new to them, a clean slate—compared to African-American congregations in one's same town or neighborhood. One virtue of working with African congregations, at least for some white churches, is that they are far, far away . . .

So it's this sort of situation—being part of the racial minority for a change, of not seeing my preferences reflected in pastoral priorities, of accepting the leadership, fellowship, and counsel of African-American Christians on a regular basis—that helps to crystallize how I've come to think about the Church, racism, and congregational formation in our time and place.

For what they're worth, here are a few of those thoughts for your consideration:

First of all, racism is not going away. I agree with Derrick Bell, the Harvard law professor, who wrote:

> Racism in America is not a curable aberration—as we all believed it was at some earlier point. Rather, it is a key component in this country's stability. Identifying vicariously with those at the top, obsessed with barring blacks from eroding their racial priority for jobs and other resources, most whites accept their own relatively low social status. This acceptance is a major explanation why there is neither turmoil nor much concern about the tremendous disparity in income, wealth, and opportunity separating those at the top of the economic heap and the many, many down toward the bottom.[4]

> Many people will find it difficult to embrace my assumption that racism is a permanent component of American life. Mesmerized by the racial equality syndrome, they are too easily reassured by simple admonitions to "stay the course," which come far too easily from those—black and white—who are not on the deprived end of the economic chasm between blacks and whites.[5]

At many points this week, we've heard about the magnitude of the things that confront us—the magnitude of racial separation in our churches, the attitudinal and perceptual gaps between Christians of different racial backgrounds (whites think racism is almost done and out the door, blacks and others think it's alive and well), the large differences in what people think racism is—how it's defined, what causes it, where to search for its remedy—and more. And it's good that we get this sort of picture—of how big and powerful and entrenched and deceptive and mystical and mundane it all is. It's good to be reminded of the dead-end that is all the racial talk in our churches and in our culture that presumes that it's all just a matter of individual attitude, opinion, or ignorance. It's good to be told that as a comparative matter, the Church has done *worse* than the American empire that so many of us criticize—we're more segregated than the public schools, than residential neighborhoods, than places of employment, than the military, than almost any other social force outside the Ku Klux Klan. It's good to have our noses rubbed in it, to have our books look flimsy and our words sound hollow. Before the Church can

4. Bell, *Faces at the Bottom*, x.
5. Ibid., 13.

expect to move forward in any significant way on matters of race, it's in need of a generous dose of cauterization, of taking fire to the deep calcifications that racism has left in the very sinews of the body of Christ.

So long as the Church remains riven by racism, it will always find itself as Cain standing before God: "Where is your brother? Where is your sister?" We remain a Church in exile, exiled by itself, unable to praise God in fullness because we have banished part of ourselves, and we continue to patrol the boundaries of banishment. And make no mistake—after all the decades and centuries of work on behalf of a world free of racism and its wrath, the harvest within the Church is so very small. As mentioned by others this week, the leading sociologist who attends to these matters estimates that only 5.5 percent of Christian congregations are at least modestly multiracial—but when you lean on those numbers, the picture gets even worse. Fully half of those 5.5 percent of congregations are merely passing through, temporarily multiracial en route to becoming monoracial places and spaces. That leaves 2.25 percent of churches in the United States—roughly 7,000 congregations out of more than 270,000. Even if those numbers are off by as much as 50 percent—not all that likely, but even if that's the case—that would still mean only 10,000 or so congregations out of 270,000.[6] More than one person has noted that it would be difficult to engineer outcomes like that even with the coercive powers of a dictatorial regime, but we've managed to do it to ourselves in the name of choice, affinity, and other considerations.

Our present situation delivers to us a variety of congregational pathologies, many of which have been explored by the plenary and workshop speakers we've encountered this week. Some of these are of newer vintage than those created by our ancestors—black, Latino, Asian, and other Christians barred from white congregations; watered-down Bibles given to slaves and the newly emancipated, forcing them to form their own congregations both in response to white exclusion and white distortion of the gospel; neighborhood congregations confronted with a changing neighborhood profile uprooting itself and moving to all-white communities; "ethnic" or "racial" congregations formed initially as a temporary measure to help newcomers or marginalized groups find their footing in the Church and society, only to be stuck in such separated realms indefinitely.

6. DeYoung, Emerson, Yancey, and Kim, "Be Multiracial," 33–43.

The newer sorts of pathologies take the larger society's confused and confusing notions on race as their starting and ending points. We see such in the operations of many "church growth" consultancies, those experts and pastors who tell congregations how to attract more members, grow their enrollments and their resources. Most of these strategies take as a given that people are most comfortable around people who are just like themselves—whites with whites, blacks with blacks, Latinos with Latinos. If you want your church to grow, in other words, strive to make it a single-race church—invite only from the ethnic group you want to maximize, try to push out those whose phenotype might confuse newcomers, and in countless other ways construct a homogeneous space in which prospective members will immediately feel relaxed, at home, and not concerned about feeling out of place or likely to confront situations of potential uncertainty or awkwardness.

At the same time, there are other church marketers—a much smaller group—who see themselves serving the niche market of people who like multiracial congregations. For a variety of reasons—they're an interracial family, being in an interracial church makes them feel they're more progressive or enlightened, they dislike the constraints of a single-race congregation—some people are drawn to multiracial congregations, or at least can be persuaded to attend such congregations.

Gayraud Wilmore, a theologian of black liberation and lifelong pastor within the Presbyterian church, notes ruefully that while "the last three General Assemblies [of the Presbyterian Church in the United States] lifted the themes of diversity and multiculturalism as the way forward," such seemed to be "mainly in the interest of church growth."[7] A denomination in numerical decline, having tried everything else, might even be willing to try building diverse or multiracial congregations as a way to stem the losses and slow their slide into cultural irrelevance.

Even among those congregations for whom multiculturalism has been part of a growth strategy, the successes are sometimes less than what meets the eye. Theologian William Maxwell notes that

> Many megachurches nationwide are boasting of racially mixed congregations. Indeed, many sanctuaries are rainbow coalitions to a greater or a lesser degree. I have visited several megachurches in Florida, Texas, and Alabama as a journalist. What I found

7. Wilmore, *Struggling Against Racism*, 32.

was this: Parishioners worship together for a few hours, but after benediction, they go their separate ways, returning to their racially segregated communities until the next Sunday, when they once again clap together, sing along together, and sway together to the music of an integrated choir.

At each church, I asked myself: has anything fundamentally changed after all these decades? . . .Worshipping together for an hour or two each Sunday is not a prescription for genuine understanding and racial transformation, not in the church, not in the society at large.[8]

One other consequence of the church-growth sort of multiracialism is one that addresses one problem by creating another—that is, by attempts to diversify a congregation racially by homogenizing it economically. Some of the megachurches that Maxwell describes fit this description, as do some of the larger and more famous megachurches in the United States—a mixed group racially, but populated primarily by the middle- and upper-middle class. The practice, if not the theory, recognizes that the sort of black and Latino folks who have best negotiated the white world, who have prospered in business or the professions, are also those best equipped to put white Christians at ease, to allow whites to worship with people "just like us" who "happen" to be black, or Mexican, or Chinese. Only in America, as the phrase goes, only in America would one of our deepest social cleavages—that of race—be thought fit to be solved by recourse to another of our deepest (and deepening) cleavages, that of class. Prosperous and successful worshipers of color are welcome—recruited, in fact—in order to build a rainbow coalition of believers whose tithes can support big parking lots, big multimedia systems, and big mortgages.

We know what passes for racial interaction and cooperation among monoracial congregations in this country—for the most part, it's summit diplomacy among pastors. In a given city or town, some pastors get together more or less frequently for fellowship, sometimes to cooperate on a project of common interest (raising hell with local authorities, for example), sometimes to support one another's church functions or projects or fundraisers. In most cases the interaction is limited to the pastors or those lay people with pastoral duties, but it is often one or more steps removed from the life of the congregation as a whole—it's just something Pastor Jones does with her time during the week, or something that Reverend

8. Maxwell, "Race and Religion," 154.

Mitchell does through a local ministerial association. In most cases, the silos remain undisturbed, mostly self-contained and self-referential and affected by churches of a different racial or ethnic profile only in marginal ways.

Still another sort of pathology, sometimes called the Constantinian theology of the church, is one we push against all the time here at the Ekklesia Project. It's a view of the Church that accommodates the Church to the state and other principalities and powers, that waters down the gospel to something that can make common cause with powerholders, that makes the church a partner in the use of violence and coercion in the service of social responsibility or justice. All of this comes at the expense of the Church's own unique mission—to be a new sort of people and new sort of human community, something of a foretaste of what God wants all of creation to be in the fullness of time. Racism and white privilege has contributed mightily to the Constantinianism of the Church at all levels.

And not just in the white churches. It needs to be said that there is a deep strain of Constantinianism in many black churches, in many churches by and for people of color. What is celebrated in some contexts as the social witness of the black church can look like a patronage machine in another; looking to secure help and favors from the state, allowing itself to become part of the mobilization mechanisms of political parties, social movements, policy coalitions, and other institutions dedicated to seeking, securing, and exercising power through the traditional means of state and market. Constantinianism poisons the gospel in the white church, and it poisons it in the black church, and it poisons it in the Salvadoran church, and it poisons it in the Korean-American church.

But one must be careful and step lightly here. That there is a deep Constantinian strain in much of the black church is something it learned from the white churches, and it is the white churches that benefit disproportionately from that arrangement. It should be a source of embarrassment and shame to white churches in the United States that black Christians for more than a century have looked to find, and have received, help and protection from the state rather than from their white brothers and sisters in Christ—indeed, that black Christians would beg the state to protect them from white Christians. Such is testimony against the Church as Church, and an indictment laid at the feet of God. Unless and until more white churches prove themselves to be trustworthy and loyal, unless and until the rhetoric of the Church as family becomes something material and tangible—affecting where we place our bodies and our money, with whom we stand and against what we struggle—nonwhite churches may be excused for thinking the state may be the main actor on behalf of God's righteousness rather than the body of Christ. Too many previous attempts have been too thin, too quickly abandoned when tested by adversity (and adversity far short of actual sacrifice or persecution); the compromises made by churches who play the politician's game reflect in no small measure the "weapons of the weak," the choices made by churches who have been rejected or ignored by their brothers and sisters in the faith.

It is this Constantinianism, I suggest, that accounts in part for the relative lack of African-American clergy and churches involved in the life and work of the Ekklesia Project. Quite simply, the notion of Church that all of us here find compelling seems implausible, unrealistic, irresponsible to many churches with nonwhite majorities. Talk of the Church as its own polis, or of the Church as the true locus for our love of and loyalty to God—all of that rings hollow to many, like theological game-playing by persons and congregations who operate from positions of relative privilege and security. While there are doubtless other contributing factors for the fact that persons of color are underrepresented in our gatherings and other projects, we need to recognize that we're paying the bills for Church practices that long predate us—many minority churches have found white congregations to be unreliable allies and fair-weather friends, and would rather take their chances playing within the space afforded them by the modern state and capitalism than to count on churches inhabited and led by the white majority. All of which makes what we do here at the Ekklesia Project even more important, even as it demands of us patience, persistence, and the determination to push toward broader and deeper solidarity among churches even against the weight of history and contemporary practices that stand against us.

But make no mistake, the Constantinian bargain exacts a price from all churches—black and white and others—who play Caesar's game. Such was the lesson learned, much to his chagrin, by the Reverend Jeremiah Wright, whose large Trinity United Church of Christ has been something of a player in the politics of Chicago's south side. Having built a large and prosperous church, able to deal effectively with government and corporate actors on a variety of concerns, the church and its leader learned some hard lessons about the state of the discussion on race and religion in America when the stakes get high.

I took the time to read and listen to Wright's sermons, the ones that prompted so much outrage from Fox News, Rush Limbaugh and his friends, and eventually from Barack Obama himself. I acquired the transcripts of Wright's major interviews and press conferences, his speech to the Detroit NAACP, and some of the other exchanges that comprised the very unusual and informative sequence of events that dominated the election news cycle during the spring of this year. What I found, of course, was that much of what Wright preached—about the violence of American power, about the conceits of empire, about the prophetic traditions of Israel and the Church—have been said by most of the pastors who find their way to the Ekklesia Project, have been said by speakers at our meetings and in our publications. But what Wright had that we don't, of course, is a member with aspirations to become president of the United States. (I don't think we have any future presidential candidates here, do we? If so, please stand up and we'll be sure to denounce you early enough to protect your electability.) Obama and his handlers showed their true colors, I'm afraid, wrapping Obama in the flag and running as quickly as possible from Wright's interruption of the assumption that Christianity and Americanism are the same thing. It was a deplorable yet entirely predictable performance by the candidate and his campaign, but one that was helpful, I suggest, in identifying the lines beyond which the mainstream will not go in allowing the Church to participate in the "public" arena. For me, the most illuminating quote from the whole exchange came from Obama himself, who at one point, perhaps tired of the whole drama, told Newsweek magazine that he doesn't go to church "to hear things that violate my core beliefs."[9]

How very American, how very enlightening of the space that political liberalism allows the Church—you can be a helpful in-house critic, but beyond that lie monsters. If Obama doesn't want his core beliefs challenged, he made the right decision to leave even a church as mainstream as Trinity UCC—doubtless he'll have no trouble finding one happy to affirm him in all he says and does.

So with all of this, with all these factors forming and deforming how the Church deals with race, we need to be honest about what won't save us, what won't solve the problem for us. It's clear that, for the Church and probably for the larger society as well, the white evangelical tool-kit, as

9. Conant and Wolfe, "Obama's New Gospel."

Emerson and Smith describe it, won't be enough. This intellectual apparatus, blending "accountable freewill individualism," the primacy of interpersonal relations in understanding social reality, and a profound antistructuralism, is such that, in the words of Douglas Sharp, the racial sociocultural order is left intact.[10]

As Alex Mikulich writes,

> Interpretations of racism as an individual problem serves white interests when whites use criticism of individual racism to alleviate personal guilt and deny their complicity in systems of privilege. Whites too often point at individual racists as a way to absolve our own [Mikulich is white] complicity in structures of white dominance. Viewing race as an individualized process obscures the ways that whites participate and benefit economically, politically, and culturally in racialized social structures. This approach reifies the ways whites learn and assume that [quoting Peggy MacIntosh] "their lives [are] morally neutral, normative, average, and also ideal."[11]

Nor will the Church's problem be solved by emphases on public policy. Segregation in the Church has survived the legal abolition of segregation in schools, in housing, in the workplace, and other public venues. If changing legal codes could have made it possible for the churches to leap the racial divide, we would have seen much more of it than we have at present.

Nor, finally, will the problem be solved for us by demographics. Gayraud Wilmore recalls a speech by then-president Bill Clinton in which the president expressed the hope that racism would be transformed when by 2050, according to one estimate, there would no longer be a majority racial group in the United States. Immigration, birthrates, and other factors would wear away at the numerical foundations of racism, finally undercutting it from below.

Wilmore notes, quite perceptively, that such a wish—that demographic change will save us from racism, at least in its worst forms—makes some rather large presumptions that don't fit with the American experience. Most significantly, Wilmore notes, is that such hopes presume that Latinos and Asians will remain outside the American black-white binary

---

10. Sharp, "Evangelicals, Racism."

11. Mikulich, "Mapping 'Whiteness,'" 107.

for racial privilege and classification. More likely, he notes, is that many Asians and Latinos (the light skinned ones, at least) "will prefer to identify with the older white majority in terms of social and political status and, perhaps, religious affiliation."[12]

Wilmore's caution reminds us that the categories of white and black are movable targets, defined and redefined and confounded by legislative, juridical, and administrative bodies—as has been true throughout America's and the world's long nightmare of modern racism. Scholars like Noel Ignatiev and David Roediger, among others, remind us about all the groups that used to fall outside the definition of "white" in the United States as recently as the nineteenth and twentieth centuries—groups that included Italians, Irish, Greeks, Armenians, Hungarians, Serbians, Slovenians, Poles, Jews, Montenegrins, Croatians, Russians, Bulgarians, Czechs, Slovaks, and more. My favorite from the not-too-distant past was an attempt by the federal government during the Depression to have Finns—people from Finland—in Minnesota defined as non-white and hence ineligible for citizenship. The argument was that Finns—and these were left-wing Finns interested in labor unions and anarchism—weren't really Scandinavian but in fact were derived from "Mongolian" ancestry, and thus could be treated legally in the same categories as low-class reprobates like Native Americans.[13]

So powerful is the black-white frame for thinking about race in the United States—think about the enduring power of the Louisiana race codes in defining who counts as black—that it's not unreasonable to see ways in which Latinos and Asians might in appreciable numbers "become white" in significant ways and for significant purposes, even as they hold onto facets of their cultural particularity for other purposes. Yet those dark-skinned Spanish-speakers from the Caribbean, for example, or brown-skinned peoples from south Asia, will almost certainly be unable to join the ranks of whiteness and reap the benefits thereof.

So demography will not save the Church either. No, if the Church is to more adequately represent and reflect what God wants the kingdom to be, it will have to be in our own way, with the tools and gifts that God gives his Church. And that gets us finally and fully into the area of formation, of making disciples, of the practices and ways in which Christians come to

12. Wilmore, *Struggling Against Racism*, 31.

13. See Roediger, *Working Toward Whiteness*, 61.

internalize the affections, dispositions, and desires of Christ in their own times and places.

And this is where it gets the most difficult—because as we've learned in our work through the Ekklesia Project, there's no simple canned program that will allow a congregation to do its job better. There's no study guide, no consultancy, no workshop that will fix the problem, address the situation, fit the local context and historical situation. But still we have to push forward, we have to keep finding ways to help churches do better what's challenging under the best of circumstances, which is to pursue the patient, persistent conversion of our lives into something that more closely reflects something of the God whom we worship and hope to follow. And race can't be just another issue or concern or problem that we tack on to an already overwhelming list of things needing our attention, because race isn't a problem out there in the world, at some remove from our churches and our common life. In fact, every effort at congregational formation is always simultaneously something that is racially formative— or deformative—in one way or another. The sooner we make our peace with that realization, even within a monoracial congregation, the sooner we'll be able to focus on what congregations well formed can do—maybe.

ECCLESIAL FORMATION AND THE NEW PEOPLE OF GOD

One reality that one encounters early on in thinking about how churches form people—or how any other social institution or set of practices forms people—is the importance of interpretive frames or frameworks: the deep rooted but generally invisible sets of assumptions, histories, categories, cause-and-effect ideas, and more that individuals and cultures internalize. These frames are what we use to order the information we receive, the experiences we have—they even help constitute what our "experiences" are—and generally provide the grid we impose on the complexity of the world in order to make sense of it. Someone with a deep understanding of the natural sciences, for example, is able to receive, process, assess, and feel moved by information and experiences in ways that someone who's clueless about science wouldn't be able to do. Interpretive frames aren't rational, propositional matters that one can easily be talked out of, nor are they generally amenable to quick replacement or abandonment.

Christian formation, when it's done well, is always a lifelong effort to push against interpretive frameworks not rooted in the word become flesh, in the Christ that brings the Kingdom of God among us and that calls us to live in the world as if that kingdom has already begun. Putting on the armor of God is as much perceptual as intellectual, as much a matter of changing the operating system of our hearts and minds as it is a matter of accepting new propositions about creation, history and destiny. It means that the process of making disciples is about taking down the scaffolding of some interpretive frames and replacing them with those of the church and the followers of Jesus—dismantling the complexes that make nationalism seem normal, subverting the conventional wisdom that might makes right, and giving people new eyes with which to see and new ears with which to hear all that's been going on around them all the while, but to which they've been oblivious so long as they lacked the right equipment with which to catch, retrieve and act upon this God-soaked reality.

This notion of "obliviousness" is key, I think, to congregational formation and the problem of race in the church. Something I found most helpful in thinking about some of this is an article by Mary McClintock Fulkerson, entitled "A Place to Appear: Ecclesiology as if Bodies Mattered." While this particular article focuses on her study of how congregations deal with people with physical and mental disabilities, it's equally helpful in exploring the church and race. She argues that a notion of the church that takes the body seriously sees the church as "a place to appear," which can be a corrective to what she calls the "obliviousness" of white, middle- and upper-class churches in regard to marginalized groups in society. She notes what most of all know, that persons of privilege—many of us, I would venture—can and have structured their lives to avoid contact with marginalized and oppressed groups in the day-to-day details of our life. Out of sight, out of mind—or, as she says, "Obliviousness is more likely to shape white, middle- and upper-middle class churches than overt oppression of the marginalized."[14]

What keeps marginalized groups of various sorts out of sight in many churches, she suggests, are all the unwritten codes that regulate bodily activity, norms of appropriate behavior of all sorts—what she calls the "incorporative practices of propriety."

14. Fulkerson, "Place to Appear," 159.

Not necessarily explicit, these norms are internalized as the respectable way to use and place one's body—from table manners, like how to hold a fork, to postures of deference or the proper ways different genders can display themselves. From the enslavement of Africans and Jim Crow laws to more recent residential, religious, and work segregation, much of U.S. society has been habituated into racialized bodily proprieties. Such practices involve the postures and gestures that are acceptable, that is, where differently racialized persons can "properly" put their bodies.[15]

Like persons in one church she studied, most white Christians have been "habituated into *a bodily sense of ownership of public or social space.* Their bodies feel comfortable in most places outside their homes; they can travel without concern or heightened self-awareness. What is produced by this practice is appropriately called 'white space,' indicating the historic dominance of whites and the continued 'spell' of that dominance even where legal segregation is passed. A mode of free and comfortable movement, this bodily propriety is possible wherever the majority of bodies are white or any black bodies present are somehow displaying 'properly' subservient postures."[16]

This is what congregational formation must do—it must surface the interpretive frameworks that lie beneath the surface of awareness, such as those involving notions of propriety, normality, comfort zones, and much else. Whether or not your church is ever integrated in a significant sense, every church needs to struggle against being something other than "white space"—that invisible ethos about which most white folks are oblivious, but which stands out plain as day to persons outside its ambit.

In one congregation she studied, Fulkerson observed that some whites complained that the church was getting "too black"—not a numerical matter, she noted, but rather a perception that there was a threat to their "bodily propriety of ownership of space." How to get beyond the realm of good intentions, making visible in our churches people otherwise removed into the realm of obliviousness, will mean different things to different sorts of congregations. Generally, however, she noted that

... what seemed to best address the inherited bodily proprieties were activities where people worked together, made decisions together, and did so in situations of shared power. The development

15. Ibid., 166.

16. Ibid., 167. Emphasis in original.

of comfort levels with those deemed "other" were crucial to shifting awareness. The face-to-face "homemaking" practices of cooking and eating, cleaning the church, sharing stories and meeting as United Methodist women all created spaces for developing empathy among members . . . . Such "togetherness" occurred on a continuum, and outcomes were not always transparent. However, these practices were "faithful to the vision" insofar as they helped diminish proprieties of ownership of space for whites, and lessen the hypervigilance of African Americans.[17]

Considerations like this—how churches construct environments of safety and comfort for members—remind us of just how much we're asking of people when we urge them to venture out of monoracial religious worlds. For black and Latino congregations, for example, we're asking them to venture outside of places where "everybody is a somebody,"[18] contrary to the messages that the political and economic world sends every day. For white and privileged congregations, we're asking them to let go of what they've been told has been their right since the day they were born—that they should always feel comfortable in each and every public setting, that what's reasonable and obvious and appropriate in their eyes is the standard to which all common enterprises must conform. For persons willing to be part of multiracial congregations, the biggest sacrifices are asked of those in the minority—less power, the need for patience and forbearance, and the willingness to deal with more, and more difficult, forms of conflict than would obtain in a monoracial congregation. People who work in multiracial congregations remind us that conflict within a common culture is generally less intense, and more easily addressed, than conflicts across cultures—not only particular incidents or dissonance, but different standards of what's appropriate and inappropriate, reasonable and unreasonable.[19] Think about stereotypes on punctuality—the obsessiveness of white Protestants compared to the mañana time of Latin cultures and the casual reality of "colored people time" by which Martin Luther King Jr. used to explain away with a laugh being late for so many public appearances.

Congregational formation on matters of race has to deal with two scenarios simultaneously—that monoracial congregations aren't going

17. Ibid., 169.

18. Everist, "Burning of Black Churches," 337.

19. See Emerson, *People of the Dream*, 145–46.

away any time soon, and that God wants us to be and exemplify something other than tightly segregated silos of the sacred. In both cases, being about the Lord's work means being about changing people's ideas of what they think they want. We're in the business of formation of preferences, desires, standards of comfort and propriety, beauty, and sin. We don't dare leave one another as the world has left us on the Church's door on day one, we're not allowed simply to capitulate to what the sociologists tell us is "natural" about people naturally wanting to be only among their own kind—indeed, the world's notions of what is natural and obvious is where we start, not where we stop. For, as we know here at the Ekklesia Project, the gospel intends to turn our ideas of nature and reason upside down, to make us capable of most unnatural behavior like loving one's enemies, turning the other cheek, giving from our substance, and much else. Of course, as a matter of faith and formation we come to see this as being more natural than what the world describes as natural, more rational—because it is in harmony with God's design of the universe—than the anemic sense of rationality that runs the world of power and violence, exclusion and domination. Grace may well perfect nature, but that doesn't mean that nature will be recognizable to the opponents of the gospel when Christ is done with it—at least not until Christ transforms them as well.

I think we need to change or supplement our language on what we think we're about when we pursue the sort of discipleship-oriented formation to which we aspire in the Ekklesia Project and elsewhere. Some of us, myself included, have sometimes used the phrase "church as polis" to describe the sort of ecclesiology that we're after—one in which the Church is our primary home, where being a Christian is that identity that takes precedence and orders all others claims on our affections, allegiances, and dispositions. The language of polis needs to be supplemented, at a minimum, by the vision of the Church as a people or race or nation unto itself—indeed, such is the vision that Paul held forth for us, and such was how the opponents of the early Church situated us—neither Jews nor Gentiles, neither Romans nor barbarians, but something altogether different. Such is more than just a rhetorical category—as the sociologist Emerson notes, people who live in multiracial congregations over time become significantly different from everybody else, so much so that he calls them the "Sixth Americans"—alongside whites, blacks, Latinos, Asians, and Native

Americans.[20] They look like an entirely different sort of racial group, at least as sociologists look at these things.

> It is not a racially homogeneous world with some diversity sprinkled in: the Sixth American's world is a radically diverse world with some homogeneity sprinkled in. It is a world, we can imagine, where one's friends, acquaintances, fellow parishioners, and perhaps even spouse, parent, or child are from multiple racial groups. It is a world where the lawyer, the bank manager, the clergy member, the construction worker, and the doctor can be of any race and often are of races different than one's own. It is a world where racially diverse others are present every day, directly shaping the lives of Sixth Americans.[21]

While none of this is easy, and much of it asks people to take risks most would rather avoid, I can tell you that change is possible, that congregations can change and reform—and not simply deform—what the embodied gathering of the faithful can be. In my own limited experience, I know that what now seems abnormal and uncomfortable is going to an all-white church. It is even more apparent in my children, for whom having to attend an all-white church seems more like punishment than a comfort zone. As we work every day to convert ourselves and our congregations more deeply into the love of God and all God's people, we may find it possible that by more adequately becoming a "house of prayer for all the nations," we'll find our ability to pray will similarly deepen and increase. That is our hope, that is our challenge, and that is our common calling.

20. Ibid., 96–98.
21. Ibid., 99.

CHAPTER 8

Whose Communion?
Globalization, Solidarity, and Communion[1]

*He or she does not belong to the universal Church in a mediate way,
through belonging to a particular Church, but in an immediate way, even
though entry into and life within the universal Church are necessarily
brought about in a particular Church. From the point of view of the
Church understood as communion, this means therefore that the universal
communion of the faithful and the communion of the Churches are not
consequences of one another, but constitute the same reality seen from
different viewpoints.*[2]

Forty years after Medellin, several decades after the irruption of the poor
into mainstream theological consciousness, ecclesiology has taken a variety of turns, engaged an increasing range of problems in the Church and
the world, and has simultaneously demonstrated dynamics of diversity (if
not fragmentation) and unity (if not homogeneity).

1. A revised version of a lecture delivered at "Transformed by Hope: Building a Catholic Social Theology for the Americas," sponsored by the Center for World Catholicism
and Intercultural Theology and the Catholic Theological Union, October 30, 2008, Chicago, IL.
2. Congregation for the Doctrine of the Faith, "Letter to the Bishops," sec. 10.

Among the topics so engaged, globalization serves as a popular umbrella concept, gathering and holding concerns in matters political and cultural, economic and theological. It requires the Church to assess matters of capitalism and borders, and the changing relations between them; questions of time and space, and how to understand the importance (or lack thereof) of place and identity; debates over the mission of the Church as a gathered, evangelizing and witnessing community pledged to continue the mission of Jesus in the world.

With such a huge topic, selectivity is required. In offering some thoughts today on ecclesiology and globalization, I will use the 1999 Post-Synodal document "Ecclesia in America" as my point of reference. This apostolic exhortation, issued by Pope John Paul II after the American bishops of North and South America examined the state of the Church and the world in the region, is noteworthy in several respects. It simultaneously suggests intriguing ways in which Catholicism in the Americas might conceive of itself in a time of global processes and dynamics, while simultaneously demonstrating the inadequacy of much contemporary Catholic ecclesiology—North and South—to provide a necessary alternative to the most pernicious aspects of globalization broadly construed.

In the brief time we share today, I would like to proceed as follows: to touch upon a few key ideas and sections of "Ecclesia in America"[3] (hereafter EA); to offer some thoughts on the strengths and weaknesses of this charter in reflecting upon ecclesiology and globalization; and to identifying some concepts, already present in varying degrees in Catholic ecclesiology in the Americas, deserving further development if the Church is to be a community with something worth saying and doing within the whirl of global capitalism, shifting practices of state sovereignty, and the interplay of cultural and human mobility.

"ECCLESIA IN AMERICA" AND ECCLESIOLOGY AFTER MEDELLIN

As one of several regional synods charged with charting a course for future pastoral and theological work, the bishops of the Americas identified themes and concerns shared by brother bishops in Africa, Asia, and elsewhere (the degree to which such shared concerns arose on their own, or

3. John Paull II, "Ecclesia in America." Further references to this work appear parenthetically in the text.

whether they were an artifact of the top-down nature of the synodal process, remains to be determined). Put simply, EA offers a straightforward diagnosis and prescription that produces a three-step process: conversion leads to communion, which leads to solidarity. Defining these terms, and specifying how they can and should relate to one another, occupies much of EA and informs both its social analysis and pastoral/political recommendations.

The document's call to conversion, of a piece with John Paul II's emphasis on a new or renewed evangelization, is emphatic that more than a casual sort of Christianity is needed both for the Church and for the world for whom Christ died. As John Paul wrote in EA, conversion

> . . . is not simply a matter of thinking differently in an intellectual sense . . . [T]rue conversion needs to be prepared and nurtured through the prayerful reading of Sacred Scripture and the practice of the Sacraments of Reconciliation and the Eucharist (sec. 27)

Further,

> [C]onversion is a lifelong task. While we are in this world, our intention to repent is always exposed to temptation. Since "no one can serve two masters" (Mt. 6:24), the change of mentality (metanoia) means striving to assimilate the values of the Gospel, which contradict the dominant tendencies of the world (sec. 28).

When the Church reclaims its emphasis on conversion—especially the conversion of those nominally in its own ranks, but also those outside the Church and the Christian family—what occurs is far from an individualistic transaction, a mere piling up of self-contained and autonomous actors. The Church itself is born and reborn in the process of conversion, making a new people distinct from all the other peoples, nations, and tribes of the world. As EA notes,

> The Catholic Church, which embraces men and women "of every nation, race, people and tongue" (Rev. 7:9), is called to be "in a world marked by ideological, ethnic, economic and cultural divisions", the "living sign of the unity of the human family" (sec. 32).

In addition:

> Through communion with Christ, Head of the Mystical Body, we enter into living communion with all believers.

> This communion, present in the Church and essential to her nature, must be made visible in concrete signs, "such as communal prayer for one another, the desire for closer relations between Episcopal Conferences and between Bishops, fraternal ties between dioceses and parishes, and communication among pastoral workers with a view to specific missionary works." (sec. 33)

Thus joined in deeper and broader ties, forged first in Baptism and sealed and renewed in the Eucharist, members of the Church are then better capable of acting in defense of the poor, in working for peace, and in confronting the realities of the American hemisphere and its marked contrasts between the powerful and powerless, rich and poor, insiders and outsiders.

This is the third category, of course, that of solidarity, what EA describes as "the social dimension of conversion" (sec. 27). Conversion leads to communion then leads to solidarity, which "makes us aware that whatever we do for others, especially for the poorest, we do for Christ himself" (sec. 26). Solidarity is that which leads the Church to seek the common good, to advocate on behalf of victims of discrimination and exploitation, and to fight against "social sins which cry to heaven"—the drug trade, political corruption, violence, and more (sec. 55).

In summary, then, the bishops of the Americas commit themselves to a dynamic and mutually reinforcing process—one may begin with either conversion, communion, or solidarity, but if healthy, one will necessarily lead to the others. They describe it in these words:

> If it is genuine, the personal encounter with the Lord will also bring a renewal of the Church: as sisters and brothers to each other, the particular Churches of the continent will strengthen the bonds of cooperation and solidarity in order that the saving work of Christ may continue in the history of America with ever greater effect. (sec. 7)

WHAT EA DOES WELL, AND WHAT IT NEEDS

For a North American ecclesiologist long concerned with Christian discipleship and the corrosive effects of capitalism on discipleship, there is much to like about "Ecclesia in America." Given the constraints of time, allow me to offer a summary rather than a detailed defense of what I see are the healthiest aspects of EA in its understanding of the Church and how such relate to matters global and transnational.

1. EA gives some understanding of how, when taken seriously, baptism and Eucharist are radical processes that create a new people and new persons. By bringing to the world that which the world cannot know on its own—Christ as the ultimate gift and revelation of God—the Church exists as a people gathered out of the particularities of nation and tribe, gender and race, even as it affirms whatsoever is good in the particularities of these identities and distinctions. In choosing the Church to continue Christ's work in the world—the priorities and practices of Jesus, the Sermon on the Mount (which John Paul called the "Magna Carta" of the Christian faith)—God offers the world an experiment that dares to suggest that forgiveness and reconciliation, rather than violence and exclusion, can create and sustain a people.

2. As an expression of the so-called "communion ecclesiology" in Catholicism, EA's understanding of the Church is capable of stressing the universal and transnational nature of Christianity. A Christian is a member of the worldwide Church as an immediate and direct effect of baptism, not simply as a member of a particular church tied to other particular churches; the social and political effects of this are apparent, especially if one takes serious the teaching of then-Cardinal Ratzinger that a person's member in the Church universal means that

> *in the Church no-one is a stranger*: each member of the faithful, especially in the celebration of the Eucharist, is in *his or her* Church, in the Church of Christ, regardless of whether or not he or she belongs, according to canon law, to the diocese, parish, or other particular community where the celebration takes place.[4]

Calls for Catholics to deport their brothers and sisters in Christ, to torture those with whom they share the Eucharist, to exploit economically those whom God has joined in one baptism and one Lord—even if for "good" reasons and even if "necessary"—seem especially problematic if the Church is what EA says it is, if it is what Cardinal Ratzinger says it is. Not only is the Church more multicultural, more pluralistic, and more diverse than any state in the Americas (or in the world, for that matter), the bonds between its members and its member churches are real and

---

4. Congregation for the Doctrine of the Faith, "Letter to the Bishops," sec. 10.

materially relevant to the life of the Church in all its aspects—worship, evangelization, and work for justice.

3. In its understanding of the Church as a communion that crosses borders, EA makes clear that living this transnational reality is not a matter for bishops or clerics alone.

> The bishops, whose duty it is to promote communion among the particular Churches, should encourage the faithful to live this communion more and more, and to assume the "responsibility of developing bonds of communion with the local Churches in other areas of America through education, the exchange of information, fraternal ties between parishes and dioceses, and projects involving cooperation and joint interaction in questions of importance, especially those affecting the poor." (sec. 37)

In so doing, EA challenges Catholics throughout the hemisphere to make real the ties of baptism that connect them with brothers and sisters they have never met, to interrupt the patterns of interaction structured for them by geography, economic position, race, and ideological affinity. Flesh-and-blood interactions with one's coreligionists elsewhere, while no panacea for the ills of the Church and the world it serves, are a necessary element in any pastoral vision that seeks to make life according to the Kingdom of God something more than a pious phrase or a cheap slogan for an otherwise thoroughly secular political agenda.

As is clear, then, I think there are several areas of EA worthy of respect and further development. At the same time, there are serious problems and omissions that undermine much of what is of value, and prevent the ecclesiology of EA from succeeding on its own terms. Let me describe a few of these.

1. While its call for a renewed evangelization and focus on conversion is an implicit recognition that all is not well in how Catholicism forms Christians, there is precious little attention to the crisis of lay formation that has undermined Catholicism in many parts of the world. This neglect of "converting the baptized," of investing the time, effort, and resources into the processes by which people move from neophytes or holders of a shallow sort of religiosity to something more robust, has contributed to the mass abandonment of Catholicism for other ecclesial communities (e.g., Pentecostalism), the wholesale ineffectiveness of the Church as a social and political voice in many societies, and the bastardization of

Christianity via unholy alliances with militarism, xenophobia, economic stratification, and more.

After a brief mention of inadequate preparation for candidates seeking Christian initiation (sec. 34), EA proceeds as if existing processes and institutions of lay formation are solid and effective. The centrality of the parish model is affirmed (sec. 41) without acknowledging the structural problems attendant to it—impersonality, its reduction to a sacramental dispensary in many places, far too many people for it to be anything approximating a community in any nontrivial sense (despite the occasional presence of parishes with many small groups that act as a "community of communities").

EA seems unduly impressed with the effectiveness of existing Catholic efforts at lay formation, especially of young people (sec. 47). I do not know whether this systematic misperception is shared widely across the Americas, but it is clearly endemic in the official documents of the Catholic Church in the United States. For confirmation, one need read no more than the U.S. Bishops' 2007 statement on "Forming Consciences" and faithful citizenship—an embarrassing document that builds its entire argument upon the Church as that which forms the attitudes, dispositions, and consciences of its members, who then take this internalized Christian *habitus* into worldly affairs. The embarrassment comes in the willful refusal to acknowledge that lay formation in the United States has collapsed, that mountains of scholarly literature point to the U.S. Catholic Church as the poster child for the abandonment of lay formation.[5] The dirty secret of Catholicism in the United States, and probably elsewhere in the Americas, is that people are more deeply formed by other institutions and processes with claims on human desires and attention—capitalism, nationalism, racial and ethnic supremacy, and much more. Without serious attention to how Christians are made—by the power of the Holy Spirit, but with the practices and disciplines of the Church—conversion becomes a momentary experience, communion is shallow, and solidarity wilts before the claims of rival gods posing as patriotism, rational self-interest, or necessity.

2. For a document prompted in part by a recognition that globalization is an important matter, EA offers no structural examination of globalization, neither in its constituent parts nor as an integrated whole. Instead,

---

5. See *Soul Searching*, by Christian Smith, for only one recent example.

one gets a list of discrete problems that may or may not be related to one another, all of which presumably are amenable to solution via piecemeal or reformist approaches that leave existing relations of power unchanged.

An ironic weakness in EA, given the fortieth anniversary of the final document from Medellin, is the later document's unwillingness to confront capitalism. Whereas the bishops in 1968 were willing to assess capitalism as an example of structural sin and institutionalized violence, the "social sins" identified in 1999 include drugs, corrupt politicians, and violence—but not capitalism. EA offers instead a critique of neoliberalism, which the bishops seem to see as a pathological form of capitalism rather than a faithful expression of it. In my view, the problems of neoliberalism are more properly seen as the problems of capitalism; a focus on neoliberalism is unhelpful, or at best a distraction, from a more adequate starting point that sees capitalism (which admits of more or less virulent manifestations, but virulent nonetheless) as something to be critiqued rather than embraced.

In this, EA follows the lead of what I consider to be the worst papal encyclical of the twentieth century on matters of economics and the church—namely, *Centesimus Annus*, released in 1991. Contrary to the wishful thinking of church liberals at the time of its release, *Centesimus Annus*—with an incoherent picture of capitalism at its center—has provided a blank check to capitalist ideologues who now list the Catholic Church as among the champions of the free market as the central social institution. If EA represents the triumph of *Centesimus Annus*, or the triumph of northern churchmen for whom critique of the capitalism that has made their countries prosperous seems inconceivable, or merely an unwillingness to analyze what seems impervious—whatever the mix of reasons, EA fails to speak effectively on globalization to the extent that it avoids or disaggregates the central engine of globalization in our time and place.

3. While the focus on Church as communion represents a true advance in ecclesiology, one with more radical potential than the bishops may recognize, EA's vision of the Church founders in its assumptions about politics and the modern state. By assuming a smooth continuity between membership in the universal body of Christ and the exclusivist claims of modern states, EA undercuts its ambitions at each stage—undermining conversion, sabotaging communion, and proffering an inadequate and contradictory sort of solidarity.

One the one. hand, this raises one of the centuries-old problems of modernity: what can it mean to be part of a worldwide communion, with material and spiritual ties to one's brothers and sisters in Christ, in a world that has actively undermined and fractured the Church in the interest of nationalism and state sovereignty? States make real claims upon their subjects (or "citizens") that brook no competition *in extremis*—killing and dying for the state and the people it purports to protect, even if doing so involves Christians killing other Christians in the name of some sectarian identity like patriotism or nationalism. In assuming that there can be no seriously conflicted allegiances between being a Catholic and being a citizen of a particular nation, EA and the ecclesiology it reflects will certainly undercut the hemispheric unity of the Church it seeks to advance.

Two particular areas of EA illustrate the confusion that arises from the disjunction between its transnational idea of Church and its uncritical embrace of state-centered politics as the arena of "solidarity." The first emerges when one looks at the roles of priest and lay person in EA's understanding of solidarity. The document notes that the priestly vocation "requires him to be a sign of unity. Therefore, he must avoid any involvement in party politics, since this would divide the community" (sec. 126). It is a curious ecclesiology that prohibits the clergy from dividing the Church, but encourages the laity to do so—yet that is what EA, following a long line of Catholic thinking, does. The laity, EA reminds us, is "best suited" to the secular world—especially to leadership roles in politics and society, from which lay people can "influence public life and direct it to the common good. In political life, understood in its truest and noblest sense as the administration of the common good, they can find the path of their own salvation" (sec. 44). So what the clergy is to build up—the unity of the Church, the Church as a communion in a material as well as spiritual sense—the laity is allowed to dismantle via the undeniably divisive operations of party politics and state policy-making. And yet we are told that the unity of the Church is the responsibility of all baptized Christians, not merely the hierarchy or clergy. One cannot hold these two views simultaneously without doing violence to consistency or hiding behind a sort of double-effect reasoning of the most ignoble sort.

Nor can one escape this tension by an appeal to the common good, inasmuch as EA's discussion of this goal doesn't specify the arena in which the common good is to be found or pursued. Is it a national, regional, hemispheric, or global matter? Is the hemispheric or global common good simply an aggregation of local and national "common goods"? Such is unlikely and inconsistent with the traditional assertion that the common good is other than a sum of individual goods. This is a significant matter at the heart of the question of the universality and unity of the Church, and what such means in a world of borders (and the changing significance of borders and state sovereignty à la globalization, regionalization, and the like).

The second collision of the state-centered view of politics and solidarity with the communion ecclesiology in EA returns us to the question of lay formation. Because for EA solidarity equates with getting states to implement policies the Church thinks serve the common good, "the Church needs to pay greater attention to the formation of consciences, which will prepare the leaders of society for public life at all levels, promote civic education, respect for law and for human rights, and inspire greater efforts in the ethical training of political leaders" (sec. 56).

In other words, while intra-church processes of forming disciples continue to deteriorate (amid untenable assumptions of effectiveness), EA calls for greater state- and nation-centered "civic formation"—with no recognition of the role that civic formation and education programs have long played in the rending of ecclesial unity in favor of nationalist projects and allegiances. Working to boost the formative power of institutions outside and often opposed to the Church seems to be a most curious sort of strategy—one may well end up with fewer politicians willing to take a bribe, but with more (if such is possible) whose primary sense of self is as a servant of the state (or "the people") rather than as a member of the worldwide body of Christ. And if the common good can only be pursued via the levers of power and by courting the powerful, one gets additional insights into one of EA's most unfortunate passages, the so-called "option for the rich and powerful," namely section 67 (which bemoans a "certain exclusiveness" in the recent past that led to neglecting "pastoral care for the leading sectors of society," thus alienating many among the rich and powerful from the Church). One cannot confront the rich and powerful with the demands of the gospel if one must court and comfort them as part of one's political strategy; nor can one seriously expect them to consider the poor as their brothers and sisters in the Church if their secular roles require them to marginalize those same poor people.

Thinking about the common good and solidarity with the poor in ways that do not privilege nationalist identities and state power requires a reorientation of imagination and agency. Last night, church leaders from the Americas offered their view of ecclesial solidarity, a concept at the center of my own work for more than twenty years; it is in advancing discussion of this concept that these brief remarks, and *The Borders of Baptism* in which they are included, are intended. Doing so, I hope, might build upon the strengths of "Ecclesia in America" while mitigating some its weaker elements.

CHAPTER 9

Whose Rationality?
Corporate Practices and the Church[1]

INTRODUCTION: CAN CORPORATIONS SAVE THE CHURCH?

"The Catholic Church in the United States is going through the greatest crisis in its history." So declares Frederick W. Gluck, former managing director of McKinsey and Company, a worldwide firm specializing in corporate consulting and management. The proximate cause of this crisis, of course, is the scandal of sexual abuse of children by priests; the inability to solve the problem, in his view, has been due to management failures within the church.

The solution, in his view, is greater reliance upon, and internalization of, corporate managerial practices in several areas: human resource management, finances, leadership, and adjustments to changed market position in the larger arena of consumers of religion. In terms of human resources, Gluck notes the problems of "insufficient talent and inadequate processes for managing it." This leadership—secular clergy and religious—is aging rapidly, its numbers are down significantly over the past forty years, it is demoralized due to scandals and conflict, and reflects the reality that "the church is no longer the first choice of the best and the brightest." Further, he laments the absence of a "performance

1. Published originally as "The Rational Shepherd: Corporate Practices and the Church," *Studies in Christian Ethics*, Vol. 21, No. 1 (Spring 2008). Used by permission.

measuring system" at any level, and the lack of a planning mechanism in terms of clerical/lay roles in the future; overall, "the church seems to lack even the rudiments of an effective human resource management process or system."

On the financial side, "the church's traditional sources of revenue are drying up," potential liabilities from the sexual abuse scandal are enormous, and church financial management systems are fragmented and uncoordinated. This corporate-consultant view of church leadership laments that "The U.S. church is a subsidiary of a large enterprise located in a foreign country where management has been historically committed to resisting change and maintaining the status quo."[2] This same national church lacks a central leadership able to drive a movement for change, this church's leadership is old and allergic to change, and hierarchical thinking dominates most thinking about how to manage. All of this exacerbates problems caused by a "potential market . . . much better informed and aware of options available to them than in the past," especially inasmuch as "many of the faithful (customers) no longer feel committed to the product line and openly reject portions of it as irrelevant to their lives." The abuse scandal has lowered the church's reputation and the market's trust in it, all of which contributes to deterioration in the church's market position.

The answer, from Mr. Gluck, is straightforward—the church should adopt more fully the sort of managerial practices and norms defined by for-profit corporations. His prescription for a "turnaround" in the U.S. Catholic Church includes a variety of financial and managerial changes, addition of comprehensive human resource policies, and similar initiatives. Doing this properly will require the creation of "an advisory board of prominent Catholic laypeople capable of devoting substantial time and effort" to the managerial overhaul of the church. The U.S. bishops should make clear to the Vatican "the absolute necessity of adopting modern management methods in the US church" as part of the turnaround strategy.[3]

Mr. Gluck is not alone in his demand for greater ecclesial inclusion of corporate practices and structures. For example, several researchers have described the inadequacy of internal financial controls in church life, leading to unacceptable levels of pilfering and embezzlement by church

2. Gluck, "Crisis Management."
3. Ibid.

people—pastors, lay staff, and volunteers.[4] A noted ecclesiologist in the United States laments that priestly formation has been altogether too "'spiritual' in nature, and needs a healthy dose of managerial training in order to equip pastors to serve the modern parish and its members."[5]

Among marketers and advertising executives, there is a widely shared sense that matters for the church would improve were Christianity given something of a "rebranding" and repositioning in the religious market via greater research on consumer preferences, demographics, and changes in church life and advertising that reflect this information.

Given all of this, it is fitting that, two years after his first article in the Catholic journal *America* referenced above, Mr. Gluck would return to offer additional advice on the necessity for a corporate revamp of Catholicism. Toward what exemplar should the church look to see how best to operate in the modern world? Gluck answers without hesitation—the church can and must learn from Wal-Mart, the goliath, worldwide discount retailer. Despite controversy over some of the firm's practices (paying unlivable wages, dumping its employees' medical and other needs on public welfare programs, unscrupulous manufacturing practices among its suppliers, rabidly anti-union ideology, and seemingly unavoidable tendencies to demolish local businesses of almost all sorts), Gluck says the church could learn many things from this corporate success story.

> With over one million employees, the Catholic Church in the United States is comparable in size to Wal-Mart, but it still follows a feudal model of governance and management . . . Such a feudal approach misses the benefits of modern management. In these days of modern communications and management, the benefits of capitalizing on economies of scale and learning in the management of human, financial and physical (land, buildings and equipment) resources are available to any enterprise with the leadership, courage and skill to make use of them.[6]

To his previous list of areas requiring corporate overhaul, Gluck adds purchasing practices (centralized rather than decentralized purchasing of everything from paper and pencils to telephone service and medical supplies, saving millions, perhaps billions, of dollars) and investment policies.

4. For example Dolbee and Sauer, "Report shows diocese's accounting system lacking"; West and Zech, "Internal Financial Controls."

5. Kress, "Priest-Pastor as CEO," 9.

6. Gluck, "Can the Church Learn from Wal-Mart?"

While he adds what seems like a pair of pro-forma disclaimers in this latter piece ("The church is not, of course, a corporation," he notes, and he recognizes that church problems "cannot be solved by better management alone"), he concludes that

> If the church is prepared to welcome the laity as full partners in important positions of authority and in key policy and decision-making bodies, the challenges of effective management will quickly be met. If the current conviction that only the clergy can play primary roles in the management of church affairs persists and the all too obvious short-comings in the church's capacity to manage its affairs continues, the current decline in effectiveness and relevance of the church will undoubtedly continue and accelerate as the clergy continues to age and replacements of equal capability and commitment are not forthcoming.[7]

By this it is reasonable to assume that it is the professional and managerial subset of the laity that Gluck intends most to empower, rather than washer-women and peasants. We'll return later to this point.

Are people like Gluck correct—is it the case that more managerial expertise and reasoning is essential to move the Church forward, to enable it to serve God's purposes in an increasingly complex social, cultural, and political world? In appraising calls for increased corporate managerialism[8] within the Church, it seems essential to assess the experiences of the recent past as part of the discernment process. This chapter, then, is a modest contribution—focusing primarily but not exclusively on select aspects of Roman Catholicism in the United States over the past few decades—to the sort of inquiry this year's conference as a whole has assumed for itself.

To state my conclusions in advance, I am persuaded that, while the Church has a great many problems, more managerial expertise and rationality as exemplified by for-profit corporations are not the solution for most of them. Rather, given its considerable formative powers—its

---

7. Ibid.

8. Definitions of managerialism abound, but MacIntyre remains a useful benchmark. To him, managerialism's claim to justified authority includes two major assumptions: "the existence of a domain of morally neutral fact about which the manager is to be expert"; and the ability to identify and utilize law-like generalizations about human and institutional life sufficient to "mold, influence and control the social environment." See MacIntyre, *After Virtue*, 77. This strong fact–value distinction is joined to an unwillingness "to think of effectiveness as a distinctly moral concept" (74).

capacity to shape attitudes, dispositions, and ways of inhabiting the world—managerialism threatens to transform the Church more than serve it, accelerating the already deep accommodation of the Church to the non-Christian world in ways detrimental to the gospel and way of life it establishes in the world. By looking at some examples of how corporate tools and complexes may work to refashion the Church into something more akin to for-profit corporate structures, we might be better equipped to contemplate the sort of forward-looking recommendations made by Mr. Gluck and his friends—and he and his friends are very powerful players in the world of Catholic politics in the United States.

INTERLUDE: SHOULD THE GOOD SHEPHERD BE RATIONAL?[9]

In choosing the title "The Rational Shepherd,"[10] I have given myself permission to explore whether making the shepherd more rational might entail draining the goodness from that same shepherd. At a minimum, it seems clear that a rational shepherd is not necessarily a good one, except perhaps in those traditions of modernity that conflate rationality (or deflate goodness) until one term defines the other. Such may well make for a better bottom line, or more sheep-per-shepherding-unit, for example, but it does seem to go against the grain of much of what we know of God as the good shepherd exemplified in the New Testament.

In fact, God as revealed in Jesus Christ seems anything but rational as understood in modernity, anything but a good steward of resources. Consider, by way of example, the many ways in which God displays a poor business model. He seems to recommend paying latecomers to the vineyard's labor the same wage as those from whom he's extracted a full day's effort (Matt 20:1–16). God seems willing to leave ninety-nine sheep alone just to recover one lost one—leaving the majority unprotected against the predations of wolves or more aggressive shepherds; at a minimum, the time spent on just one sheep could obviously be put to better use—increasing the size of the flock, or perhaps diversifying out of shepherding into another sector (Matt 18:12–14). What looks to be God's personnel policy may generate public relations benefit (for employing the "differently abled"), but recruiting the poor, the lame, and the marginalized (Luke

9. This section derives from Budde, "God is Not a Capitalist."

10. The original title of this essay. See n. 1 above.

14:12–14) is not how a rational actor builds an enterprise. The quality of human capital matters greatly, after all, talk of stones the builder rejected notwithstanding.

Other manifestly irrational policies seem to typify the God that Jesus conveys—promising persecution and perhaps martyrdom to those who get the corporate message right (e.g. Mark 13:7–13; Luke 9:23–26), putting the first in last place, not charging for healings, miracles, or loaves and fishes, and much more. God seems unaware that this management approach leads inevitably to bankruptcy: either God wasn't being literal in ways binding on the rest of us (our preferred reading, in most cases), or else God needs sober-minded lower managers to protect God's patrimony from God's overly generous heart. That would be our job, of course, in most understandings of all of this—as in a business where layers of functionaries protect the enterprise from the profligate generosity of the kindly but out-of-touch founding patriarch, now reduced to a figurehead role.

One may object, of course, that all of this describes God, and we are certainly not God. Such is both true and trivial, especially if it allows us to evade the deeper point and questions of how to read Scripture communally in these contexts. Christians have long believed that whatever we conclude God to be or not to be should have some significant influence on what we as the Church should or should not be. If God is merciful, the Church should not be extortionate. If God loves enemies, so should the Church practice enemy love and reconciliation rather than vengeance and retributive bloodlust. While God's mission does not rely upon the Church perfectly acting as God acts, direction does matter and similarity does matter, making the Church's imperfect witness of today a herald of the eschatological fulfillment promised in the Lord's time. And while one may not be able to derive a "theology of organization" directly from the New Testament, no theological approach to such concerns can be wildly at odds with the picture of God in Christ offered therein.

So, one crucial consideration among others when assessing the utilization of for-profit tools and norms in Church life is whether such allows the Church to witness to this most unusual sort of God—one for whom profligate generosity and self-emptying bankruptcy is constitutive of God's own self. It does not rule out *ab initio* all learning from non-Christian sources, but it does suggest that one test of such innovations is whether they help form Christians capable of giving as God gives, and shepherding as God does. Does the Church redefine "rationality" in ways consonant with this good and generous Shepherd, or does the rationality of modernity redefine the gospel in ways more conducive to itself? Might it not be the case that the most "rational" shepherd in the gospel drama is the much-maligned Caiaphas, a religious manager par excellence, whom crisis forced into recommending the death of one for the good of the people (John 18:14)? To these sorts of questions we shall return later.

THE FORMATIVE POWER OF MANAGERIALISM

Elsewhere I have examined several cases in which adoption of for-profit corporate practices has done violence to ecclesial aims and aspirations. The church's embrace of advertising and marketing has given us the licensed use of the image of Pope John Paul II for a brand of potato chips and pre-paid telephone cards. The encroachment of so-called "death corporations"—giant conglomerates that are fast taking over thousands of funeral homes, cemeteries, crematoria, and the like—has led some Catholic diocese to enter into dubious partnerships with such firms, while other dioceses have stayed independent but adopted several of the conglomerates' questionable tactics.[11] More recently, product placement has entered the picture, as the Walt Disney Company created a contest that offered a thousand dollars and a trip to London to a pastor who mentioned "The Chronicles of Narnia" in a sermon during the film's promotional period—pastors had only to submit their sermon to Disney to be entered in this drawing. In a similar merger of corporate promotion and congregational life, General Motors sent singer Patti LaBelle and a fleet of Chevrolet SUVs into fourteen African-American megachurches for inspections and test drives.[12]

Beyond these sectoral cases stand some larger, more significant questions. It may well be that managerialism's most potent threat to the Church flows from what can only be described as a contest of formation between them. Both seek to shape the affections, dispositions, and desires of their disciples, both make definitive claims about the nature of reality and human existence, and both require that other loyalties and allegiances

---

11. See Budde, *(Magic) Kingdom of God*; Budde and Brimlow, *Christianity Incorporated*.

12. "Product Placement in the Pews?"

be oriented to them in an inferior or subordinated fashion. To the extent that the sort of rationalism embodied in corporate managerialism dominates within Church life and practice, to that extent will the church shrink in significance and importance as a divinely gathered people charged with heralding and prefiguring however imperfectly the inbreaking Kingdom of God.

The formative powers of business managerialism are impressive precisely as they seem mundane in our day. As noted by John Haughey,

> the main influences on business conduct are affections that have been generated by the world of business itself. Growth, productivity, efficiency, the bottom line, being competitive—these are constitutive aspects of the Western business enterprise. But they can also be seen as affections. The objectives of the business enterprise frequently become affections . . . One can go from being efficient as an objective to internalizing efficiency as an affection . . .[13]

Paul Hessert notes how the phenomenon of money, and its centrality in our world, itself is a profoundly formative force. Our monetary structure, he says,

> . . . trains us to think in certain ways. It is derived from the fundamental notion which first generated money and then was universalized by money, that "reality" is quantifiable, that it can be divided into identical units and so be measured, compared, and manipulated.[14]

This is a matter of great significance, he notes, inasmuch as money as universalizable quantification is a concept and abstraction that, although a convention, forms the world in determinative ways. "'Everything that exists exists in a measurable quantity' is the creed of our culture," he writes. Such a convention is profoundly important to theology inasmuch as it structures the distinction between "inner" and "outer" in modernity.

> What is quantifiable, and because it is quantifiable, is subject to the universal mediation of money, is "real". Those things which elude this kind of quantification are "spiritual"—love, loyalty, tradition, courage, honor, family, pride, and the like. There is no common unit which brings these two different realms together.

13. Haughey, "Affections and Business," 688.

14. Hessert, "Theology and Money," 629.

Quantification, by dealing with certain aspects of life, identifies these as real and outer. By the same means, quantification isolates a realm called "inner" and "spiritual," designating it (by default) as less than real. Religion does not so much challenge this structure in order to give an independent validity to the spiritual. Rather, it supports quantification by accepting at face value its own province of the "spiritual" which quantification relegates to it. In other words, religion in our culture legitimates this quantified and secularized version of reality.[15]

That a specific notion of quantity and measure forms not only the professionals but the modern world is recognized by some scholars within professional disciplines themselves. Accounting scholar I. C. Steward notes the social power that accrues to managerial and business professionals to define objectivity, expertise, and reality.

Accounting practice is framed by an overarching metaphor of numeracy. The columns of figures with their dual structure and mathematical accuracy create a presumption that the accountant's work is objective, that the accountant is representing reality "as is" through the use of [numbers] that are objective and value free. The profit and loss, for example, is not thought of as a "mere" matter of interpolation, dependent on the accountant's perspective, values or skill. The accountant is paid not merely to provide his/her point of view on the profit and loss status of the firm, but to state the objective facts of the matter.[16]

Steward quotes another business scholar, Gareth Morgan, who notes how "the numerical view highlights those aspects of organizational reality that are quantifiable and built into the accounting framework (for example, flows of costs, revenues, and other values), but ignores those aspects of organizational reality that are not quantifiable in this way." Morgan further notes that:

Just as we might attempt to rate the quality of last night's meal on a scale of 1–10, and in giving it a "9" capture that it was indeed a very good meal, the accountant's numerical form of representation provides a very "thin" and limited characterization. It leaves much of the quality and overall experience of the meal out of the

15. Ibid., 630, 632.
16. Stewart, "Accounting and Accountability," 635–36.

account. The metaphor "it was a 9" remains silent on so many things.[17]

Steward describes how the power of numerically constructed reality is reproduced and transformative within corporate life. "[R]outine operation of the organization's internal accounting systems, for example, people, students, patients, and work teams, become profit centres generating revenues and expenses. Where financial considerations become a major issue, the data generated can exert a decisive influence on the accountant's reality construction."[18]

Managerialism constructs and participates in a metaphysics of naïve realism, of modernity's relegation of religion to the internal and disembodied, and a specious fact/value distinction that empowers those capable of defining the factual, the real, and the objective. This metaphysics also funds and spreads through colleges and universities in which economics (the "queen" of the social sciences) and professional business training stand as formative bodies in their own right.

The notion of humanity as self-interested and endlessly acquisitive—a bedrock assumption of capitalist economics and business education—itself turns out to be a self-fulfilling prophesy when one considers that the process of studying economics and business (and affiliated professional fields) may well make students more self-interested and unethical than they were before beginning such studies, and than are those of their contemporaries who pursue other passions.[19] As noted by Jacques Ellul many years ago, far from being more resistant to such socialization processes, the highly educated (including those in business and professional programs) seem to be formed more deeply by them, having willingly immersed themselves in the routines and structured reinforcements of educational systems longer than people with less schooling.[20]

Robert Brimlow notes the similarities between the sort of formation conducted in professional education schools and what used to typify ecclesial practices. As he notes:

17. Ibid., 636.

18. Ibid., 636, italics original.

19. For some of the general issues and research, see Ghoshal, "Bad Management Theories"; Aspen Institute, "Where Will They Lead?"; Frank, Gilovich, and Regan, "Does Studying Economics Inhibit Cooperation?"; Pfeffer, "Why Do Bad Management Theories Persist?"; Collins, "Voluntary Brainwashing."

20. Ellul, *Propaganda*.

The period of study, trial, and initiation resembles the preparation of priests and ministers: the professional schools operate as proto-seminaries. Indeed, the very term "profession" originally referred to the taking of vows by religious responding to clerical vocations, vows which could only be taken after years of postulancy and no-vitiate—analogs to internships and probationary employment. The study pre-professionals engage in parallels biblical study: there are certain sacred texts which characterize the professional fields—the basic and serial scriptures which outline and describe the history and development of the fields. And there are the "covenants," or codes of professional conduct, which are binding and normative, i.e. they prescribe and proscribe behaviors, define excellence and determine value for the members of the profession.[21]

In all of this, Brimlow notes, "professions are paganistic in their ritual practices: in the ways they govern not only the business activities but also the familial and affective lives of their members; and in the way their members come to view themselves."[22]

For these reasons, one should not draw too much hope from the increased number of professional development and academic programs aimed at improving the managerial capabilities of Church personnel and leaders. Among the best of these in the United States is the Center for the Study of Church Management, founded in 2004 by the School of Business at Villanova University, an Augustinian university in Philadelphia. This Center is devoted to "the study and application of sound business methods to Church decision making," according to its founding director, Charles Zech.[23] It offers educational programs and conducts research in the areas of administration, professional financial management, and human resource management as they apply to the Catholic Church and its institutions.[24]

The Center's programs range from one-day topical workshops to weeklong summer certificate programs and an online Master's degree in church administration. The Center is developing an M.S. in church management, which it envisions as an entirely online experience save for a

21. Brimlow, *Paganism and the Professions.*
22. Ibid.
23. Center for the Study of Church Management, "Director's Message."
24. Center for the Study of Church Management, "About the Center."

residential learning experience at the beginning and end of the program.[25] The Center emphasizes the concept of "best practices" in church management, and plans to highlight such cases and norms via its newsletter and other initiatives.

In many ways, then, this Center should be well positioned to make worthwhile contributions to the effective integration of corporate managerial practices into the operations of the Catholic Church. And, in fact, it seems likely to do so—its advisory board includes bishops, church bureaucrats, and corporate leaders (especially but not exclusively in finance and management consulting). Its faculty program committee draws heavily from Villanova's School of Business, especially in the areas of accounting, management, finance, and marketing.

And yet, when one inspects the course work offered by the Center, one finds little other than a standard business curriculum that targets church agencies rather than business entities. The formation, in other words, is corporate and empiricist from start to finish—there seem to be few or no opportunities to form the liturgical, spiritual, or ecclesial aspects of church employees, managers, and leaders. The Center seems to presume that the church has already well formed the leaders and employees sent to the Center for professional development; it similarly seems to presume that persons interested in a career in church management need no such ecclesial formation before running churches and church-related institutions. Managerial and administrative skills alone seem to suffice.

Standing behind all of the specific formative capacities of business schools, professional training, and corporate life itself, are the broader formative processes of capitalism. The advertising and marketing practices discussed previously are themselves part of a larger cultural ecology that shapes desires, affections, and dispositions in deep and far-reaching ways. Even if one restricts oneself to a cursory examination of the cultural power of for-profit culture industries (advertising and marketing, television and radio, print media and the internet, and more), one gets a taste of the structures and processes that aim to form persons and the categories through which they inhabit the world and the Church.[26]

The statistics are so familiar as to fade into insignificance, while in fact they are crucial in understanding the world in which we live. People

25. Center for the Study of Church Management, "Center Programs."

26. Portions of this section derive from Budde, *(Magic) Kingdom of God*, and Budde and Brimlow, *Christianity Incorporated*.

in advanced industrial countries spend more hours of the day engaged with for-profit culture industries (television, radio, film, online providers) than they do anything else, except work and sleep. Young people in the United States spend well over twenty hours per week watching television and engaged with digital amusements of various sorts. A major study by the Kaiser Family Foundation discovered that multi-tasking among cultural products exposed children in the U.S. ages two to eighteen to six and a half hours per day of media products; young people aged eight to thirteen averaged more than eight hours per day in a mediated sea of predominantly commercial media.[27] Adult statistics on the whole are not much better. What all of this entails, as many people have explored elsewhere, is that the desires, affections and dispositions of people in late capitalism are shaped in deep and profound ways by the formative aspects of for-profit culture industries and the cultural ecology they construct.

Compared to the saturation of symbols, stories, songs, and images delivered by corporate culture industries, the Church's efforts at forming its people in determinative ways seems decidedly inadequate. Again, the studies are too well known as to need recitation. For mainstream congregations, Catholic and Protestant, in most of North America and western Europe, lay formation is an underfunded, neglected, and often token exercise. It ignores adults in favor of children, generally abandoning even the pretense of engagement by the early teen years; it tends toward the individualistic and subordinates itself to more powerful and presumably more important loyalties—to the state, to middle-class ambitions, and to the market.

The capacity to form anything more than nominal Christians takes more time than the vast majority of mainstream churches and their parishioners are willing to invest. The majority of Catholic church-goers in the United States (who are themselves more engaged in ecclesial life and formation than those who do not attend) spent virtually no time engaged in church life beyond the act of Sunday liturgy. In the course of a year, most Catholics in the United States will read no books about their faith (historical or contemporary, about its social teaching, etc.), subscribe to no Catholic or Christian periodicals—will do nothing, in other words, to broaden or deepen an adult appropriation of their faith. The problem goes beyond a lack of information about one's faith tradition—in itself, that is

27. Roberts et al., *Kids and Media*.

not new. Rather, what is lacking is a matter of fluency and internalization of what it means to think, feel and desire as a Christian.

The failures of Christian faith formation are noted in many studies, most recently and notably by Christian Smith, whose important book *Soul Searching* even uses the practices of Catholicism in the U.S. as his empirical case for lay formation at its most inadequate.[28] Other scholars have documented similar phenomena, but Smith's theological and ecclesiological acumen makes his study especially valuable.

Given this—the power of managerial and corporate formation, buttressed by the formative nature of a culture in which commercially driven appeals are everywhere—it seems clear that the tools of rationalism look to be more powerful than the formative capacities of the gospel. What that means in practice is that the tools and those who wield them, far from being in service to the gospel and the Church, are more likely to conquer and transform them.

Does It Matter? Organizational Theory, Ecclesiology, and Christian Ethics

How one conceives of the Church—as supernatural or human construct, as similar to non-ecclesial bodies in significant ways or qualitatively different—explains much of the variation in whether and with what degree of confidence Christian ethics embraces corporate managerialism or not. Among those ecclesiological traditions that posit strong distinctions between the visible and invisible church (the latter escapes full structural expression, reducing the significance or centrality of the former in significant ways), the Church need not worry excessively about the effects of managerialism upon its institutional life.

As explored by Clare Watkins,

> In this ecclesiological tradition the relating of any organizational or management theories to the church depends on an understanding of the institutional Church as an attempt at a structural expression of the mysterious, essentially undefined, community in Christ. In the last analysis, however, the ecclesia "as a body of

28. Smith, *Soul Searching*.

> Christ . . . has nothing to do with an organization and has nothing
> of the character of the institutional about it"[29]

Watkins sees much of this sort of ecclesiology as derived from the work of Emil Brunner, being carried through liberal Protestantism throughout the twentieth century. As Watkins reads Brunner, "the Church is still to be seen as structurally special, but not radically separated from other human structures. This allows for the practices of management in the Church under the direction of certain theological assertions."[30] This notion of visible/invisible Church in Brunner itself presupposes a more relaxed understanding of sin, a greater appreciation for points of contact between revelation and the human and created order, and a more optimistic doctrine of providence. The visible church merely assists the non-Christian world to learn what the world can probably learn on its own anyway, so it is both appropriate and uncontroversial for the Church to organize itself in ways congenial to secular norms.

A contrasting view of the Church leads to a more circumspect approach to management and corporate tools. This latter view, evident in Barth and Catholic theologian Yves Conger (among others), makes strong claims that the church is a special sort of institution, brought into being by the work of God with structures and purposes unlike those of other institutions. It emphasizes the single nature of the Church rather than seeking recourse in visible/invisible distinctions, and takes seriously the notion of the Church itself as part of God's revelatory action.

> An ecclesiology which wishes to assert that certain aspects of ecclesial structure are "ontologically anterior" [Congar's phrase] to the community would appear to have some problems in employing management science in the ecclesial realm. In this case the institutions themselves are so radically bound up with the divine that managerial analysis and reform would be inappropriate.[31]

Such a statement must be qualified, of course, inasmuch as theologians like Barth and Congar were identified with Church reforms of various sorts; what must remain unchanged, however, is the notion of the

---

29. Watkins, "Church as a 'Special' Case," 374; quoting Brunner, *Misunderstanding of the Church*, 11.

30. Ibid., 374.

31. Ibid., 371–72.

Church as a community of people called into a distinctive way of life, the visible and material quality of which is not accidental or contingent.

This visible/invisible segmentation of the Church is of a piece with the unhelpful dichotomies of inner/outer and sacred/secular mentioned previously as cause and consequence of modernity. As noted by Javier Martinez, Catholic Archbishop of Grenada, the implications for Christianity are significant:

> [A]s soon as the sphere of the religious, in which Christianity as a whole is placed, designates a particular sphere of human activity next to other spheres (philosophy, morality, the sciences, the arts, and so on), it is thereby severed of any other human reality; it becomes autonomous, but it has to become unreal also, since to every parcel of reality corresponds its own sphere of knowledge . . .
>
> To religion there is no reality left, and therefore it cannot be even a kind of knowledge, it has to belong to the purely private and subjective realm of sentiment and preference. Its concern, if it is conceded that is for something "real," has to be for a wholly otherworldly "reality."[32]

Not surprisingly, conventional organizational and management theory is more compatible with ecclesiologies that de-emphasize the special nature of the Church, and in fact seem to reinforce trends that minimize the Church as part of God's revelatory action in the world. One of the most common expressions of this is to see the Church as part of "civil society," the category in modernity that is neither state nor market, and in which political and social thinkers of many types have invested their hopes for human improvement. Actors in the realm of civil society are supposedly able to provide social cohesion, norms of communal solidarity, and insulation against the corrosive effects of capitalism and the modern state.

Indeed, given this ecclesiology, it would be "irresponsible" not to embrace the best of corporate practices—not to do so would grant this visible, historical church a distinctiveness and importance it does not merit, because Christianity itself need not be seen as all that distinctive. To reject this open ecclesiology would be to consign the Church to premodern irrelevance and mediocrity, precisely at a time when the tools—corporate managerialism—for relevance and expertise are more readily available than ever before.

32. Martinez, "Beyond Secular Reason."

Nonprofit organizations are key to the importance of civil society in much of this literature, and indeed the Church itself is commonly thought of as a nonprofit organization itself these days. Designating the Church as such—as a voluntary organization of like-minded people who join together in a common interest or pursuit of common tasks—situates the Church as a useful part of the public order, serving the nation by providing goods and services beyond the confines of Church membership. Equating churches with nonprofit organizations is a distinctly Protestant notion in the modern era, specifically an expression of the rise of denominationalism in ecclesial and public life. As noted by Craig Van Gelder:

> The inherent logic of a denomination is that it is organized to do something, normally doing something on behalf of God in the world. It is essentially functional in its identity and purpose. This follows the logic of organizational sociology. An organization when it is formed must seek to accomplish some goal. Building on the foundations of free-church ecclesiology, denominations and their congregations were formed around a functional and organizational rationale.[33]

Among the foremost voices in management theory as applied to the Church, at least in North America in the twentieth century, Peter Drucker stands out. Considered the founder of managerial theory in a career that spanned six decades and influenced everything from how scholars and practitioners think of leadership in corporations to the restructuring of the Japanese auto industry after World War II, Drucker has had a significance influence on the thinking of many church people as well. In addition to his consultative work over two decades with Rick Warren, author of *The Purpose-Driven Life* and a founding force in the evangelical megachurch movement, Drucker has helped form large numbers of church pastors and administrators through a variety of institutional vehicles and books.

One book of relevance here is *Managing the Nonprofit Organization: Principles and Practices*, published in 1990. In this book he uses churches and nonprofit organizations interchangeably with one another, and makes churches part of the larger universe of nonprofit organizations capable of learning from the actions of other nonprofits. Nonprofits of all sorts, according to Drucker, "exemplify and fulfill the fundamental American commitment to responsible citizenship in the community . . . . We now

---

33. Van Gelder, "Rethinking Denominations," 26.

realize that [the nonprofit corporation] is central to the quality of life in America, central to citizenship, and indeed central to the values of American society and of the American tradition."[34] While he once envisioned the large capitalist firm as the locus of community in the years after World War II, he now looks to nonprofits in general and churches in particular as supplying this need—the latter seen not as religious entities, but as social bodies providing communal centers for an otherwise fragmented culture.[35]

Reinforcing the centrality of formation in matters of management, Drucker notes that:

> The "non-profit" institution neither supplies goods nor controls [as do businesses and government]. Its "product" is neither a pair of shoes nor an effective regulation. Its product is a changed human being. The non-profit institutions are human-change agents. Their "product" is a cured patient, a child that learns, a young man or woman grown into a self-respecting adult; a changed human life altogether.[36]

Drucker's approach is focused on helping corporations of all types see the importance of mission statements, tailoring their work to specific and achievable goals, and creating "value" for customers rather than simply maximizing profits. Indeed, another founder of the megachurch movement, Bill Hybels of Willow Creek Community Church, once kept a poster outside his door with the Drucker maxim: "What is our business? Who is our customer? What does the customer consider value?"[37] An ecclesiology that gives people what they want, that defines would-be adherents as customers, that defines the Church as a business, is one in which managers and pastors embrace in a pact of growth and good feelings. This disposition to using market research to customize the Church fits well with Drucker's emphasis on the rise of the "knowledge sectors" of society, which requires that nonprofits assume greater chaplaincy responsibilities in modern life; at the same time, churches themselves are filled

34. Drucker, *Managing the Nonprofit Organization*, xiii.
35. Stafford, "Business of the Kingdom."
36. Drucker, *Managing the Nonprofit Organization*, xiv.
37. Twitchell, "Jesus Christ Superflock."

with people working in and formed by knowledge sectors, and in need of care and counsel themselves.[38]

Perceptive critics like Eugene McCarraher have noted the idealized, almost romantic, picture of corporate life that Drucker paints in his work.[39] Such a rosy picture of corporate managerialism as empowering employees rather than manipulating them, creating an ethos of cooperation rather than exploitation, appears among Drucker's admirers as well. But among some of his admirers—too few, however—there is an acknowledgement that Drucker's picture of corporations as embodying a healthy and affirming balance of objectives depends on profitability, prosperity, and the lack of competitive pressure.[40] It is a luxury, in other words, rather than constitutive of corporate practice.

All of this, of course—the diminished significance of the visible Church, the positioning of the Church as a subset of civil society and an example of one sort of nonprofit organization among others—comes into question when one seeks after a more robust ecclesiology that sees the Church as something akin to God's "demonstration plot" in the world,[41] a people called by God to embody a new form of human sociability not built upon exclusion or violence. This view of the Church, taking its "mission statement" from the priorities and practices of Jesus as related in the Gospels, recognizes "the corporate character of the church, expressed in such language as 'people of God,' koninia, 'body of Christ,' 'covenant people,' 'household of faith.' It is this character of the church which makes it also a place for moral formation."[42]

Among other things, this sort of ecclesiology resists the repositioning of the Church as a nonprofit organization, and its reduction to an element of civil society. Civil society in general, and nonprofit organizations in particular, are creatures of the state, defined by the modern state for specific purposes and that exist at the pleasure of the state. Far from the idealized contractarian notions of civil society giving rise to the state, as an historical matter the causality is generally opposite—states create civil

38. Stafford, "Business of the Kingdom."

39. McCarraher, "Money is the Root of All Order," 46–47.

40. McCann and Brownsburger, "Management as a Social Practice," 513.

41. Hays, *Moral Vision of the New Testament*, 97.

42. Rasmussen, "Ecclesiology and Ethics."

society and set its parameters.[43] A Church that willfully redefines itself as a nonprofit entity created by the state and in business to serve society as a source of cohesion, trust, and fellow-feeling, I would suggest, is not a Church but a chaplaincy.

In contrast to the notion of Christian ethics derived from the sort of Brunnerian ecclesiology mentioned by Watkins—a translation exercise that seeks commonality between worldly norms and Christian "principles"—Arne Rasmussen makes Christian ethics intrinsic to the Church as a special sort of institution unlike any other on earth.

> That the church is a place for moral formation and discernment means that the church, with its common practices, symbolic world and moral training, is a prerequisite for right Christian discernment. . . . Ethical discernment thus requires training, the shaping of character. And this is a communal process. . . .
>
> Ethics is then nothing else than discipleship, sanctification, spiritual life, or however one wants to describe the Christian life. It has to do with the whole of life and not with specific universal duties, and no sphere of life is outside of it. In this sense, Christian ethics is inevitably a theological ethics (in contrast to autonomous ethics); it is embedded in the whole network of Christian convictions, practices, rituals, and dispositions.[44]

The formative practices of the Church, in other words, are primary and ought to go deeper than those associated with any other discipline, including that of corporate managerialism. Indeed, Christian formation aims to offer a construction of what is "real" and "realistic" in ways that other institutions—profit, nonprofit or otherwise—cannot, and indeed often find unhelpful as they seek to realize the operationalizations of their mission statements, goals, and initiatives.

More Managerialism?

All of which is well and good, but what might it mean for discerning how to think about future recommendations to increase the breadth and depth of corporate managerialism in the life of the Church? Let us examine one proposal in particular, one in fact associated with multinational

43. See, for example, Cavanaugh, "Killing for the Telephone Company."

44. Rasmussen, "Ecclesiology and Ethics," 184.

management consultant Frederick Gluck, with whom we started our time together.

Gluck is part of a powerful network of Wall Street investment bankers, corporate lawyers, management consultants, and corporate leaders who have joined multimillionaire investor Geoffrey Boisi in forming the National Leadership Roundtable on Church Management. This group of prominent and wealthy corporate leaders has embarked on an ambitious plan to bring the latest in managerial expertise and corporate "best practices" into the life of the church at all levels—from parishes and dioceses to the level of national bishops' conferences. Their project has found allies in many quarters of the church bureaucracy, including several dozen key American bishops and several Catholic journals of opinion and commentary. The Leadership Network claims to have no interest in changing church doctrine or policy, but instead seeks a greater leadership role for lay expertise in managing church operations and functions.

Via a series of conferences, publications, consultancies, and media initiatives, the Leadership Network seeks to improve church administrative procedures at all levels. It has entered into a partnership with the Archdiocese of New Orleans on matters of Catholic schooling, and it aims to spread its vision of "best practices" in human resources, finance, and management throughout church entities at all levels. Doing so, according to the Network's leaders, will allow the church to benefit from lay expertise and experience drawn from the corporate world.

How should one view such an initiative? It may be significant that two commentators as dissimilar as Eugene McCarraher—a Catholic social historian and self-described socialist—and Richard John Neuhaus—a champion of Catholic neo-conservatism in politics and economics—would find common ground in being troubled by such a mobilization among Catholic corporate executives and philanthropists. Boisi et al. seem to exemplify that sort of bureaucratic-managerial takeover of Catholicism, under the guise of "lay empowerment," that McCarraher explored in a piece entitled "Smile When You Say 'Laity': The Hidden Triumph of the Consumer Ethos" in 1997.[45] Neuhaus has recently expressed fears that the purported neutrality of this wealthy group is a smokescreen for a liberal assault in favor of issues like the ordination of women and married people.[46] One

45. McCarraher, "Smile When You Say 'Laity.'"
46. See Neuhaus, "Checks, Balances, and Bishops."

wonders whether Neuhaus's concern is not for rich people shaping church policy, but that these are not his kind of rich people—Geoffrey Boisi and not, for example, conservative billionaire Tom Monaghan. Still, both seem skeptical that expertise can in fact be "neutral" in effect and eventually in intent, and that calls for greater efficiency may in fact be nothing more than a grab for power.

How can the Church discern a path forward in all of this? One modest suggestion would be for the Church to conceive of itself as something of a cultivator of *poesis*, a community in which tools and talents are consistently and routinely kept in service to appropriate ends—in this case, embodying the gospel in a people called to discipleship in the world.[47] Can the Church see management tools—from the mundane to the revolutionary—as intermediate goods that must not be allowed to occlude or redefine ultimate goods? Such would take seriously MacIntyre's caution about the ongoing tension between practices and the institutions necessary to sustain them even as institutionalization constantly threatens the integrity of those very practices.

Such an approach would take more seriously the power embedded in corporate managerial practices—far more seriously than is evidenced by their practitioners and those among us who take their disciplinary and formative powers for granted. To use an old category, a church alert to the dangers of managerial power might approach innovations and changes with a risk standard similar to that confronting pharmaceutics (at least in theory) in the United States (unsafe until proven safe), rather than a surgical model (safe until proven unsafe).

Taking the formative powers of managerialism seriously might impose a set of requirements for persons presuming to "modernize" or bring "expertise" into church life. A mantra in such circles is that church leaders—bishops, priests, clerks, volunteers—all need professional development, training, workshops, and immersions in order to be rational and efficient leaders. But if the goal is to keep shepherds good and not merely rational, perhaps business leaders and corporate consultants, and those employing the skills of business and administration within the church, should be required to submit to intensive, lifelong Christian formation as a prerequisite for serving the Church. One wonders how many of Boisi's power elite would agree to a regular and intensive regimen of long

47. See McCarraher, "False Gospel of Work"; on this point, thanks also to members of the Liturgical Identities Seminar in Christian Scholarship at Calvin College, July 2007.

retreats, Scripture study, direct practice of the works of mercy, and other "inefficient" and intrusive practices before being unleashed on church agencies and personnel. These exercises in Christian formation should be constructed preferably by religious communities and traditions not usually disposed to corporate chaplaincy, in order to provide at least some distance and critique of the fundamentals of power (and not simply its incidentals and event-specific ethical questions). Without such a transformative experience—without attempting to "convert" the baptized among corporate executives and thousands of low- to mid-level managers in the church—such powerful persons will likely be unable to keep the Church and its agencies discernibly "Christian" in any worthwhile sense, will be unable to keep means from redefining ends and instead becoming agents of the further diminution of the gospel in our day. In fact, such a series of discipleship-forming practices for corporate leaders and experts might become an invaluable prototype for a more comprehensive commitment to lifelong lay formation within the Catholic tradition and others in which Christian formation has been a neglected and faltering practice. Such would seem to be essential in order for the Church to begin to define a notion of rationality that is distinctively Christian in inspiration, of ends and means rightly joined in faithfulness to the gospel, rather than one bunkered in the liberal canons of modernity. Whether such a notion of "ecclesial rationality" might be possible or worthwhile, of course, presupposes the creation of a people capable of communal discourse and discernment distinct from that of business-school socialization.

Were something like this to be tried, were the contested politics of formation both recognized and resolved in favor of privileging one's baptism over one's role in the managerial hierarchy, one might see steps toward keeping the shepherd good and not merely rational. An altogether new sense of "best practices" might yet emerge, in which the generosity of God finds reflection, however incomplete, in the common life of those who aim to be disciples of Jesus.

CHAPTER 10

Treason and Allegiance:
Martyrs, Anti-Martyrs, and the Gospel[1]

INTRODUCTION

Political authorities, in punishing the transgressors the Church would narrate as "martyrs," have not generally described their actions as making martyrs. Frequently those on the sharp side of the sword found themselves condemned as traitors—to the empire, the clan, the state, or the people. Historian Lacey Baldwin Smith draws attention to the frequent and close links between martyrdom and treason, even as the distinctions between them often seem arbitrary[2]; martyrs "recognize a higher allegiance and on occasion are happy to betray the loyalties that lesser men and women hold sacred . . . "[3]

Joyce Salisbury, among others, suggests that the earliest Christians were turned in by their neighbors for reasons that were "shockingly simple."

> Christians were perceived by their pagan neighbors to be antisocial in the deepest meaning of the word. They were creating their own society within the Roman one, and their loyalties were to each other rather than to the family structures that formed the

1. This chapter also appears in Budde and Scott, *Witness of the Body*.
2. Smith, *Fools, Martyrs, Traitors*, 6.
3. Ibid., 15.

backbone of conservative Roman society. Their faith led them to renounce parents, children, and spouses, and Romans believed this actively undermined the fabric of society. In fact, it did.[4]

It may well be that the charge of treason weighed less heavily on the consciences of Christians in the first centuries of the Church than on later ones. While Christians under Rome prayed for the emperor and avoided outright rebellion, they harbored no sense that it was *their* empire, that they had a crucial stake in sustaining and empowering the regime through their participation and support. The empire was a fact of life that sometimes brought them good or ill—akin to the weather—but seldom did the early Christians lose sight that they were part of a more important community, a polity with claims upon their loyalty and conduct far deeper than those of Caesar. The Church was their true polity, a community called out from the diversity of human cultures to be a foretaste and harbinger of the Kingdom of God. Their citizenship rested in heaven rather than in Rome; having the empire accuse one of treason might be unpleasant but it was not seen as surprising, nor did it often engender the sort of inner turmoil typical of deeply divided loyalties.

The Constantinian/Theodosian settlement removed wholesale persecution of the Church from the equation, but it sharpened rather than resolved the tensions within Christian thought and practice on political authority, obedience, and Christianity. Such tensions inhered in the odd reality of texts often read as counsels to political subservience and obedience (e.g., Rom 13:1–7, 1 Pet 2:13–14) being written by persons themselves often imprisoned for disregarding imperial and local orders. How could Peter and Paul have ever become martyrs if they had acted in accord with the sort of mandatory obedience later Christians derived from their New Testament texts?

Since Constantine, Christians have long been confused about what to do when presented with evil or unjust regimes. Some authorities, on scriptural and/or natural law grounds, maintained that believers were to submit meekly even to the worst of regimes. Others argued that regimes that violated the Church or minimal standards of justice had thereby voided the rule of obedience owed by Christians, while others counseled submission until powerholders at other levels (e.g., local magistrates) moved against those in power. The legacy of this confusion grew even

4. Ibid., 16.

more complex during the modern era, with the addition of considerations of just revolution (derived from just war theory) and liberation pushing against the conservative biases of earlier accommodations and norms. Neither the counsels of obedience nor the defense of revolution, for the most part, saw the Church as a people or polity in its own right, distinct from clan, state, social movement, or nation. Those within the Church that maintained this sort of ecclesiology were marginal in their communities, or else prosecuted by their coreligionists on charges of treason.[5]

Nevertheless, martyrs continue to call the Church back to a stronger sense of its own uniqueness and distinctiveness. Just as Christians have long studied and venerated the lives of the martyrs in order to deepen believers' journey of discipleship, so may other lessons and exemplars emerge from reflecting on what I call "anti-martyrs"—persons who put other loyalties above their membership in the body of Christ, who refused martyrdom in favor of personal advantage or accommodation. Anti-martyrs may be of several types. Some are persons whose primary loyalties are to a state, ideology, or movement rather than to the gospel of Christ. Others are those who betray their Christian brothers and sisters in exchange for inducements, incentives, or advantages. I would exclude from this category persons who abjure the faith as a result of torture or extreme fear—such people testify to human finitude and weakness rather than to an affirmative privileging of an identity superior to that of being a Christian. While such distinctions may become obscured in the messiness of human conflict, I believe they retain value as interpretive categories.

This chapter explores some twentieth-century examples of martyrdom—and anti-martyrdom—in order to offer some observations about discipleship, secular allegiances, and membership in the transnational body of Christ. In doing so, I hope to contribute to a disarming of the power of "sedition" or "treason" as an accusation leveled against Christians. For too long, Christians have sought to deflect charges of treason, bending over backward to prove their loyalty and reliability to rulers of all sorts. Instead, I think the integrity of the Church and its faithfulness to the gospel are better served by resituating "treason" as an irremovable possibility of a robust ecclesiology that "seeks first the Kingdom of God." It is likely the case that Christians understand "treason" in ways distinct from how it is understood in conventional political terms. If Christians

5. See Gregory, *Salvation at Stake*.

can overcome the squeamishness attached to accusations of disloyalty, they may find themselves better positioned to be better followers of Christ and able to serve "the welfare of the city" (Jer 29:7) in ways the city needs but refuses to accept. Such is always important, but perhaps especially so in our era, marked as it is by fluctuating ideas on obligation and loyalty, and shallow modern and postmodern confidence in multiple, overlapping, and hybridized identities and allegiances.

A Tale of Two Archbishops

No one envisioned that the cautious and bureaucratic Oscar Romero, the "safe" choice to lead the Archdiocese of San Salvador in 1977, would soon be proclaimed a martyr by Christians worldwide—indeed, such is part of Romero lore and the stories told about him.

Romero became archbishop during a dark period in El Salvador's one-sided civil war, in which government and affiliated military groups did the vast majority of killing in a conflict that led to tens of thousands of deaths. The regime and its death squads targeted anyone seen as sympathetic to reform efforts benefiting the poor, whether in urban or rural contexts—union organizers, advocates for land reform, human rights workers, religious educators, and church leaders defending the dignity and priorities of the poor. The death squads that pushed Romero into public opposition to the regime—a stance that included weekly homilies describing atrocities and abuses (which drew ratings higher than any radio broadcasts except World Cup soccer[6]), cancelling all masses except for the funeral Mass of a Jesuit murdered by the government, and more—also killed Romero. On March 24, 1980, Romero was gunned down while saying Mass, executed by a death squad run by the founder of El Salvador's now-ruling party and a graduate of U.S. military training (Roberto D'Aubuisson, founder of ARENA, and a champion of several right-wing groups in the U.S.). The assassin's bullets hit home a day after Romero called upon soldiers to stop the repression of the poor, and after he issued a public appeal to U.S. President Jimmy Carter to cut off all funding to the Salvadoran military.

In 2005, timed to coincide with the twenty-fifth anniversary of Romero's murder, the Vatican announced the opening of beatification

---

6. See Kravel and Wilkinson, "Assasinated Archbishop."

proceedings on the archbishop's case—the first step toward possible formal proclamation of sainthood in the Catholic tradition. The canonization of Romero, as well as his proclamation as a martyr for the faith, has been politically charged from the moment of his murder.

The Salvadoran government has consistently resisted characterizing Romero as a martyr, claiming instead that he died as a leftist partisan in the civil war. Far from being a witness to the Christian faith, many elements of the Salvadoran elite then and now viewed Romero as a communist sympathizer who subverted Church and state alike. Similarly, most of Romero's fellow bishops (and Vatican officials like Cardinal Alfonso Lopez Trujillo) maintained that Romero did not die for the faith but rather because of his misguided leftist sympathies.[7] Indeed, during his brief time as Archbishop, many of Romero's fellow bishops and the Vatican nuncio to El Salvador sought to silence or replace him.

Among the majority of Christians in El Salvador and elsewhere, however, Romero died as a martyr rather than as an ideologue. Throughout the region, at the level of popular piety Romero has been received as a pastor whose defense of his flock led him to embody Christ's sacrifice anew. Romero was no mere propagandist for the political left (whom he critiqued and about whom he harbored significant misgivings), but someone who testified to the power of Christian love and discipleship in life and death.

Ironically, despite efforts by Vatican bureaucrats to derail or slow the process of Romero's canonization, the slain leader has enjoyed the support of two significant figures: Pope John Paul II and Pope Benedict XVI. As noted by Paul Jeffrey, "John Paul clearly believed Romero died a martyr for his faith." During a 2000 celebration commemorating twentieth-century martyrs, John Paul was upset not to find Romero's name on the list of Christian martyrs compiled by Vatican officials; John Paul wrote in Romero's name himself, and added that Romero was "killed during the celebration of the Holy Mass."[8] The former Joseph Ratzinger, now Pope Benedict XVI, told reporters in 2007 that Romero merits beatification (the first step in canonization) and acknowledgement as a martyr for the faith.[9]

7. See Jeffrey, "After 25 Years."
8. Ibid.
9. Winfield, "Religion in the News."

Halfway around the world, another Catholic archbishop faced another dictatorship willing to kill clergy and lay leaders it considered to be subversive. His story ended very differently, the last act being played out on a world stage with a surprise ending.

At the start of the Mass installing him as Archbishop of Warsaw in January, 2007, Stanislaw Wielgus stunned the dignitaries packing his cathedral—and viewers watching the live broadcast—by resigning from the position. Two days earlier, after weeks of denial and evasion, he admitted to having worked with the Polish secret police for many years during the Communist era.

Wielgus agreed to become an informant after he requested permission to study abroad in the late 1970s. While Wielgus insisted that he turned over no information of value to the secret police, a church commission concluded that "numerous essential documents exist that confirm Rev. Stanislaw Wielgus' willingness for conscious and secret cooperation with the security organs of Communist Poland."[10] Polish newspapers reported that he informed on dissidents and priests for more than twenty years, and perhaps met with police more than fifty times in one five-year period.[11]

Despite the Catholic Church's opposition to communism in Poland and the Eastern Bloc, Wielgus was not the only church leader to have collaborated with internal security forces. Father Tadeusz Isakowicz-Zaleski, a priest who attempted to organize a Solidarity chapter in his seminary before being stopped by his superiors, was tortured by Polish secret police (who videotaped the session for subsequent instructional purposes). Twenty years later, when reading the five hundred-page file the police had compiled on him, Zaleski learned that two priests were among those who informed on him.[12] When his superiors refused to look into the matter, Zaleski began his own research on church leaders who collaborated with the secret police.

What he found in secret police files once believed to have been destroyed was that between 10 and 15 percent of clergy in the Archdiocese of Krakow were police informants or collaborators. While the information in such files is notoriously uneven in reliability—the police often

10. Associated Press, "Warsaw Archbishop."

11. Smith, *Fools, Martyrs, Traitors*, 6.

12. Hundley, "Tortured Priest's Tenacity."

included rumor or outright falsehoods in attempts to discredit people or boost their own image of effectiveness—Zaleski identified thirty-nine clergy (five of whom were bishops) whom he believes cooperated with the regime. Historians familiar with the Polish case estimate 10 to 15 percent of clergy nationally were informants or collaborators, comparable to Zaleski's figures for Krakow.[13]

After having attempted to inhibit discussion of clergy collaboration, the Polish bishops established their own commission to review secret police files. While noting the unreliability of the files and the need to corroborate information therein, the bishops' commission noted that of one hundred and thirty-two bishops living in 2007, "about a dozen were registered by the security services of communist Poland as 'secret collaborators' or 'operational contacts,' with one described as an 'agent' of the intelligence agency."[14] The commission's report was forwarded to the Vatican for review.

While the existence of collaborators does not detract from the church's reputation for having resisted the communist regime, it does raise questions in at least some respects. Not all collaboration was extorted via force, nor from blackmail (despite recent revisionist attempts to attribute nearly all cases to brute coercion); and denying someone permission to study abroad does not compare with torture and beatings used to elicit collaboration. It is possible that at least some collaboration came from persons who believed such was their civic duty to cooperate with the official organs of government. Ironically, the regime's most successful period of recruitment seems to have been during the 1980s, the era of Solidarity and the papacy of Karol Wojtyła, who was spied upon by several priests over a period of years.[15]

THE SACRISTAN AND THE PRIEST

On October 26, 2007, the Catholic bishop of Linn (Austria) and the Archbishop of Innsbruck announced the formal beatification of Franz

---

13. Ibid.
14. Associated Press, "Polish Church Reports."
15. Luxmoore, "Secret Policemen's Bishop."

Jägerstätter, whom they described as a "martyr" and "a prophet with a global view and a penetrating insight."[16]

These bishops' predecessors had a very different view of Jägerstätter and his witness, however—indeed, the church's about-face on this Austrian farmer testifies to the power of even the most seemingly useless of gospel-based witness. Had Jägerstätter's case not come to the attention of the Church worldwide, thanks largely to the scholarly work of the late Gordon Zahn—had his memory remained within the confines of the Austrian church alone, in other words—it is hard to see this parish sacristan as someone who would later be praised and a martyr and candidate for sainthood.

What Jägerstätter did, he did in the face of opposition from all sides—from his mother and wife and family, his friends and neighbors, his parish priest and bishop, and of course from his government leaders. After returning home from basic military training in 1941, Jägerstätter vowed not to return, refusing to help advance the Nazi cause as a member of the Austrian military (Austria had been annexed by Germany in 1938). He considered Nazi Germany to be an evil regime wholly incompatible with Christianity, describing its wars as unjust plunder and savaging of its neighbors which his Christian conscience could not allow him to support in any way. Despite repeated efforts on all sides, Jägerstätter refused to change his mind; he was arrested and finally executed by beheading in 1943.

While Jägerstätter's position rested on the duty to follow Christ rather than an evil regime bent on the destruction of the innocent (as well as of the Church), his pastors emphasized that such decisions were not the responsibility of lay persons. Rather, they were to obey civil authority in accord with Romans 13 and similar texts; they also emphasized Jägerstätter's duty to provide for his family, who would be made to suffer if he continued to refuse military service to the Nazis.

In one of his letters, Jägerstätter observed:

> If people took as much trouble to warn men against the serious
> sins which bring eternal death, and thus keep them from such
> sins, as they are taking to warn me against a dishonorable death,
> I think Satan could count on no more than a meager harvest in
> the last days. Again and again, people stress the obligations of

16. Schwarz and Scheuer, "Foreword," 1.

conscience as they concern my wife and children. But I cannot believe that just because a man has a wife and children, he is free to offend God by lying (not to mention all the other things he would be called upon to do). Did not Christ Himself say, "He who loves father, mother, or children more than me is not worthy of My love"? Or, "Fear not those who can kill the body but not the soul; rather fear much more those who seek to destroy body and soul in hell"?[17]

In his research on Jägerstätter, including interviews with his family and neighbors, Zahn described the general sense of the community about Jägerstätter, both during his lifetime and when his witness began gathering international attention after more than a decade of silence.

[T]he community continues to reject Jägerstätter's stand as a stubborn and pointless display of essentially political imprudence, or even an actual failure to fulfill a legitimate duty. It is to be explained and forgiven in terms of an unfortunate mental aberration brought about, or at least intensified, by religious excess. The question of whether his action was morally right is, for the most part, set aside. While some of the villagers were quite willing to accept the possibility that he might someday be formally acknowledged as a saint, this possibility was not considered at all incompatible with the community's general disapproval of his action.[18]

Zahn notes that, for the most part, Jägerstätter's contemporaries tried to avoid talking or thinking about him—his story was not told to their children, and most seemed to hope the story would go away on its own.[19] When it came to Catholic leaders, Zahn notes that while "they could congratulate him for his unswerving commitment and give him assurances that he would not be committing a sin . . . none had been able or willing to tell him that *he was right*."[20] In fact, many in the Austrian hierarchy after the war had difficulty discussing Jägerstätter's case in ways that didn't reflect poorly on their support for the war effort.[21] Emblematic in this respect, to Zahn, was Bishop Joseph Fleisser of Linz, who after the

17. Zahn, *Solitary Witness*, 97–98.
18. Ibid., 146.
19. Ibid., 146–48, 150.
20. Ibid., 162.
21. Ibid., 164–65.

war could describe Jägerstätter as a "martyr to conscience" but not as an example worthy of imitation.

> I consider the greatest heroes to be those exemplary young Catholic men, seminarians, priests, and heads of families who fought and died in heroic fulfillment of duty and in the firm conviction that they were fulfilling the will of God at their post just as the Christian soldiers in the armies of the heathen emperor had done.[22]

Jägerstätter, then, was a rather curious martyr, one whose witness was "a stand *against* his fellow Catholics and their spiritual leaders who were wholeheartedly committed to, or at least willing to acquiesce in, the war effort."[23] This powerful and improbable witness dramatized what one English bishop (during the Vatican II discussion of what would become the Pastoral Constitution on the Church in the Modern World, *Gaudium et Spes*) described as "the major scandal of Christianity," namely that "almost every national hierarchy in almost every war has allowed itself to become the moral arm of its own government, even in wars later recognized as palpably unjust."[24] How ironic, then, that Bishop Fleisser's successor would be among the bishops describing Jägerstätter as "a prophet with a global view and a penetrating insight . . . an advocate of non-violence and peace."[25]

A generation later, thousands of miles away (but in a place itself touched by Nazi immigrants and fugitive war criminals), another Catholic presented a witness quite different from Jägerstätter's refusal to cooperate with an evil regime. His came during the dark years and military repression of Latin America, which saw the entire region after 1954 fall to dictatorship, death squads, and authoritarian civilian regimes. In many countries, the Catholic Church and its leaders resisted such U.S.-backed regimes and their policies.

Such was not the case in Argentina, however, where almost all church leaders supported the dictatorship and its "dirty war" between 1976 and 1983; during this period, tens of thousands were abducted, tortured, murdered, or disappeared. Argentine bishops provided information

22. Ibid.
23. Ibid., 162–63.
24. Ibid., preface.
25. Schwarz and Scheuer, "Foreword."

to the regime about their own priests and lay leaders, defended the regime publicly against international and internal criticism, and called on the Christian faithful to support the regime in its fight against godless Communism.[26]

In October, 2007, a Catholic priest received a life sentence for aiding the junta in seven murders, thirty-one cases of torture, and forty-two kidnappings. Christian von Wernich served as a police chaplain during the dirty war; while he is the first priest prosecuted for human rights violations in Argentina, human rights groups suggest he was far from alone in committing such violations.

Witnesses in von Wernich's trial testified that he listened to the confessions of prisoners, turning over to interrogators the names of persons mentioned during the sacrament of reconciliation. In addition, von Wernich questioned detainees, was present during torture sessions, and dealt with and misled family members searching for persons abducted by the state.

He also provided moral support to the torturers and killers among the Argentine military and death squads. As one officer stated, "Father von Wernich saw that what had happened had shocked me and [he] spoke to me, telling me that what we had done was necessary; it was a patriotic act and God knew it was for the good of the country."[27]

The "patriotic acts" of torture and murder defended by von Wernich were directed, in most cases, against persons who shared his (and the torturers') Catholic faith. In siding with the state over against his core-religionists, he even violated the absolute confidentiality of sacramental confession. In a church unable to distinguish between the body politic and the body of Christ, von Wernich was loyal to the former and a traitor to the latter. In this, von Wernich reflected the view of many Catholic dictators throughout the region—that the church had become infested by Marxist subversives and dupes. In killing and torturing church leaders, in other words, the faithful Catholics in the government, military and death squads were purging the church of anti-Christian elements that had corrupted it—they persecuted the church in order to save it, in other words.

In this, the Argentine and other dictators were joined by many members of the Argentinian Catholic hierarchy. Archbishop Adolfo Tortulo,

26. See Mignone, *Witness to the Truth.*

27. McDermott, "Interrogator in a Cassock"; see also Usborne, "Argentina's Disappeared"; Burke, "Argentine Priest"; Barrionuevo, "Argentine Church."

head of the military vicariate and president of the Argentine Bishops' Conference, took time during episcopal meetings to justify torture on theological grounds derived from medieval sources. His successor as head of the military vicariate, Bishop Jose Medina, concurred in his defense of torture.[28] Beyond their defense of torture and other atrocities, according to attorney Emilio Mignone, the military vicariate provided other essential services that describe a general practice that was to play out in the particulars of von Wernich's case:

> Above and beyond particular abusive incidents, the main role of the chaplains—who took their orders from the military vicariate—was to distort and soothe the conscience of repressors, by legitimating violations committed against the dignity of the human person. "When we had doubts," Admiral Zaratiegui has said, "we went to our spiritual advisors, who could only be members of the vicariate, and they put our minds at ease." They went so far as to compose sacrilegious prayers. One of them goes, "Impart skill to my hand, so the shot will hit the mark."[29]

Not only did the junta derive consolation from church chaplains like von Wernich, it also drew ideological support from bishops like Victoria Bonamin, to whom the world was divided between "atheistic materialism" and "Christian humanism"—the latter defended by the dictatorship.

> The antiguerrilla struggle is a struggle for the Argentine Republic, for its integrity, but for its altars as well . . . This struggle is a struggle to defend morality, human dignity, and ultimately a struggle to defend God . . . Therefore, I pray for divine protection over this "dirty war" in which we are engaged.[30]

BOTH PERSECUTOR AND MARTYR?
THE STRANGE CASE OF GABINO OLASO

In an October 12, 2007, column, noted Catholic journalist John Allen described the unusual background of Father Gabino Olaso Zabala, an Augustinian priest and one of 498 martyrs of the Spanish Civil War beatified by the Vatican in October, 2007. What makes the martyred Olaso

28. Mignone, *Witness to the Truth*, 4, 7, 9.
29. Ibid., 11.
30. Quoted in ibid., 6.

distinctive is that, forty years before, he committed heinous deeds in the service of the Spanish empire.

In 1896, Olaso participated in the torture of Father Mariano Dacanay, a Filipino priest thought to be sympathetic to anti-Spanish nationalists in the Philippines. Held in the Augustinian seminary in Vigan, Dacanay was tortured by guards who received encouragement and assistance from Olaso; according to Dacanay's subsequent account (generally accepted as credible, according to Allen), Olaso himself kicked Dacanay in the head, rendering him semi-conscious.[31]

While Catholic theology does not require that persons proclaimed as martyrs must have lived pious lives—dying for the faith not restricted exclusively to moral exemplars in life—Olaso does present some rather strong contrasts. But unlike Saul the persecutor whose allegiance to Christ made possible Paul the martyr, Olaso's nationalist allegiances remained unchanged throughout his life. What he was willing to torture for he was apparently willing to die for—a consistency that raises as many questions as it answers. St. Augustine, in whose name Olano served as a priest for decades, famously proclaimed that Christian martyrs are distinguished not by their manner of death but by the cause for which they died (noble pagans can die bravely under adversity, but to Augustine only dying for the true faith makes a Christian martyr). One wonders, in that case, about interpretations of the "cause" capable of justifying the torturing and martyring of a fellow priest (in a seminary, no less) and the subsequent martyrdom of the torturer himself. One cannot help but wonder whether Olano lived a defective notion of Christian discipleship, distorted by the toxin of nationalism, or whether he was a faithful modern follower of Augustine, who defended the torture of the Donatists as an act of charity aimed at saving them from perdition—or whether the two positions are identical.

Learning from Martyrs and Anti-Martyrs

In diverse ways, these cases offer insights to persons concerned about Christian discipleship in our day. By pushing against the legacy of a presumed identity between Christianity and political loyalties, these exemplars contribute to greater clarity in vision and practice.

31. Allen, "Torture in his History."

As noted by many scholars,[32] the power of martyrdom generally requires the existence of a church or community capable of receiving that witness—to name and affirm it, reflect upon and disseminate it, to employ it as a model of Christianity well lived that is taught to others. In the cases of Romero and Jägerstätter, such a church was missing in part (El Salvador) or altogether (Austria) during the martyr's lifetime. It took the larger Church—transnational, not beholden to a single set of national allegiances or commitments—to recognize and receive the martyrs' witness. Such may well be a structural commonplace in the era after modernity, with the worldwide character of the body of Christ sliced into national fragments; tied so closely in many places to nationalist fusions of faith and political identity, such churches may be less capable of recognizing martyrdom in their midst (unless persecution comes from the outside, targeting the "patriotic believer" on both grounds).

Jägerstätter provides a martyr's witness against Austrian Catholicism nearly as much as against Nazism. His refusal of military service asks uncomfortable questions of ecclesiastical, political, and cultural forces that chose to cooperate with the Germans. And while Romero was immediately proclaimed a martyr by popular voices within the Salvadoran church, such a view was rejected by most of his fellow bishops, the papal nuncio, and powerful Catholics tied to the regime and its backers in El Salvador and the United States. Left to themselves, the churches in Austria and El Salvador would probably have suppressed or rewritten these martyrs' stories such that their witness would have either remained invisible or been rendered harmless. To counteract the structural shortcomings of national churches requires the entire Church, able and willing even to proclaim some martyrs as a means of fraternal correction of local churches.

One thing distinguishing suicide from martyrdom, according to Craig Hovey, is that while the former often tries to control the meaning and power of one's death, martyrs entrust themselves

> . . . to the church's memory with no guarantee that the church will discern the meaning of their death in its continued existence. This is not because they might be betrayed by the church but because even in death they openly subject themselves to the church's discipline. After all, the way the church narrates the past is a work of disciplining its tendencies toward self-deception and learning

32. E.g., Salisbury, *Blood of the Martyrs*, 2–3.

> to speak truthfully, especially about those things at which it has failed.[33]

Having stood for the Christian way even in the face of substantial church opposition, in other words, Jägerstätter and Romero also bought their brothers and sisters a chance to repent and speak truthfully even at a remove of several decades.

For many people, some of these cases pluck the strings of moral intuition long thought dormant or diminished in an egalitarian age. For some, the heinous acts of von Wernich and Olaso (and the betrayal by Wielgus) are worse because they are ordained clergy; similarly, the sacrifice of Jägerstätter is all the more remarkable because he was a layman, not a cleric. Whether a remnant of the dual-ethic thinking of Christendom or residual clericalism, these cases invert our moral anticipations—we find martyrdom more consistent with the totality of commitment presumed by the clerical vocation, and the willingness to torture more likely among lay persons whose vocations more frequently legitimate the use of lethal and coercive force.

The wrong way to engage this moral intuition is to ascribe it to a presumption of innate virtue among clerics rather than to the lay state. More appropriate, I believe, is to recognize in it the stirrings of a guilty ecclesial conscience left over from the compromise with lethal force in Christendom (in which lay persons could kill when necessary, but such was eventually considered to be incompatible with the ordained state). The shock of clergy as killers, torturers, and collaborators, whatever else it does, forces us to ask why we feel as much disquiet over the status of the doer compared with the deed itself. Is torture by lay Christians a lesser offense than that of Olaso or von Wernich—if so, why?

Similarly, and despite the more recent celebrations, Jägerstätter's choice disquiets in ways that similar choices by a cleric would not. Jägerstätter's refusal was not in the midst of a life of clerical celibacy and limited personal obligations, but rather in the midst of all the "natural" responsibilities of fatherhood, marriage, community, and locality—all the things, in other words, that historically have "excused" lay people from following the way of the Cross unto death if necessary. Priests and nuns can give their life for Christ because they do not have spouses, children, and neighbors who depend upon them (married Protestant clergy represent

33. Hovey, *To Share in the Body*, 51.

an interesting category of persons pulled in opposite directions); a milder version of discipleship has been seen as appropriate for lay persons, in which being reasonable and cautious is both appropriate and legitimated. Jägerstätter's isolated witness upends this comfortable compromise, bringing back Jesus' unambiguous words on family and discipleship to all Christians—ordained and lay, married and single, young and old.

Hovey is correct in noting the deep continuities between martyrdom and the spiritual/ecclesial practices and disciplines that attach to all Christians who understand their baptism.

> [M]artyrdom is not at the far end of a continuum marked out by various degrees of self-denial. It is not asceticism to the extreme, penitence with greater intensity, the most uncomfortable hair shirt imaginable. Instead, "deny yourself" is related to "take up your cross and follow me" as means to end. The former is necessary to accomplish the latter. The way of Jesus requires the unseating of those modes of behavior, ways of life, desires, and thoughts that are conditioned on scales of self-preservation, self-protection, and security for one's life. The church upholds its commitment to the way of Jesus when it helps members undergo the discipline necessary to resist the lure of wealth and cultivate the imagination required to reject vanity, the humility to ignore temptations to feed the acquisition of power, the patience to wait for justice when wronged and the courage to withstand harm without the soothing consolation of revenge. The virtues necessary to be a martyr are no different from the virtues necessary to be a faithful Christian. This means that martyrdom is not a special calling for a select few but the commitment of every Christian and the responsibility of every church. Even though not every individual Christian will be killed, there is no way to distinguish those who will from those who will not. Even though not every Christian will be remembered as a martyr, every church that locates its identity in the cross is obligated to cultivate those virtues necessary to enable all of its members to die for the cause of Christ. Every Christian is a member of a martyr-church.[34]

The scandal of the anti-martyrs raises another question of which is the worse offense—treason against the state, or treason against the Church? Not only did the three anti-martyr pastors explored here (Olaso, von Wernich, Wielgus) serve their respective regimes, they did so in ways

---

34. Ibid., 59–60.

that targeted their coreligionists. They informed against their brothers and sisters in Christ, used their sacramental roles against the faithful, and put national allegiance over the ties of baptism. In this they were joined by the murderers of Romero and other church leaders, for whom the state represented the true protector of Christian values against a Church rendered unworthy of respect or allegiance.

This question of betrayals chosen—state or Church—may in the future present itself more frequently and in more diverse forms than one might imagine. For example, the use of government informants and spies in congregations is likely to increase as a result of some church leaders' refusal to cooperate with laws affecting ministry and pastoral care among undocumented immigrants—an example of what one conservative commentator calls "philanthropic lawlessness" as a gentler substitute for the term "treason."[35] More plain-speaking patriots decry what they see as "aiding and abetting the criminal invasion of America by Mexicans."[36] Infiltration of churches, and of congregants informing on one another and pastors, are foreseeable both because of the more pronounced anti-immigrant views of white Christians in the United States as compared to church leaders,[37] and because of the longtime fusion of Christianity and nationalism in the U.S. church. Being loyal citizens in these cases will be a more powerful motivator than inhibitions against betraying fellow Christians; indeed, so deep is the presumed identity between the two in American culture that such a possibility is denied in principle by most people. Standing with "America" cannot mean standing against the Church, only against a misguided and corrupt version of Christianity temporarily in charge. The affinities between U.S. and Latin American rationalizations of anti-church religious nationalism (subverting the corrupt Church and its leaders in order to protect "true" Christianity) are unmistakable.

CONCLUSION: THE PECULIARITIES OF CHRISTIAN TREASON

Christian treason is a most unusual sort of thing, at least when compared with traditional political and secular understandings of the term. Christian treason does not arise from fealty to another state or worldly

35. Levitske, "Illegal Immigration."
36. Ovadal, "Romanizing America."
37. See Smith, "Attitudes Toward Immigration."

sovereign, but to the Prince of Peace, whom the Bible portrays as a contrast to all worldly principalities and powers. In this, the children of darkness may perceive more accurately than do the more optimistic children of light; the more optimistic persist in thinking that kings and rulers, regimes of all types, actually might want what Christ wants if only they were more enlightened.

There is no simple formulation or rule that will suffice for dictating when Christians must obey God rather than human authority; searching for such a rule or checklist itself adds to the problem by removing the discernment of situations and choices from the gathered body of the Church. For churches that take themselves seriously as forerunners of God's new creation, as an eschatological community whose common life and witness to the Kingdom of God is something distinct from the capacities of the nations, the consistency of their corporate existence likely makes state action the variable factor at issue. In a way, Ronald Reagan's explanation of his move from the Democratic Party to the Republicans provides an imperfect analogy—he didn't leave the Democrats, in his view, but rather the party left him by changing its priorities and commitments. Such may well describe the ebbs and flows of when discipleship becomes treasonous for churches with a sense of themselves—their life and practice remains the same, with secular powerholders moving the goalposts separating acceptable and unacceptable conduct and thought in accord with state needs and aspirations. What is unexceptional in one context—loving one's enemy, naming the names of killers, offering help to the poor—becomes subversive when the lines separating secular loyalty and disloyalty are moved by the powerful.

Too much emphasis on "treason" itself can obscure the more important point that, for Christians, the more fundamental category is one of loyalty—to the gospel, to continuing Jesus' work as the Kingdom of God continues to unfold, to the brothers and sisters in the church, and to those whom Jesus calls us to love in spite of the world's logic to the contrary. What the world narrates as treason is merely a season in the larger story of Christian allegiance to something larger, deeper, and more real than the political claims of states and sovereigns. If the Resurrection ultimately deprives death of its sting (1 Cor 15:54–56), perhaps the creation of the Church at Pentecost will ultimately deprive accusations of treason of the power to undermine ecclesial solidarity and Christian practice.

CHAPTER 11

The Borders of Baptism:
Formation and the Custodians of Death[1]

For a long time I used to think that only old Trotskyites called people
"comrade" any more. Then my father died. A well-known business and
political figure in our home town, my father drew a crowd even in death.
More than a thousand people filed past his casket, many standing for
hours in a line a block long. The procession of friends, relatives, and well-
wishers seemed relentless; a six-hour parade of consolations, encouragement, and reminiscences. Despite the solemnity of it all, it was a fairly
noisy affair; and unavoidably so, given the size of the room and the numbers of people.

The noise stopped and the line froze late in the day as a group of men
from the local American Legion post assembled at my father's side. These
had been his friends and cronies as young men; as old men now charged
with witnessing to one another's passings, they adopted a military bearing
once second nature to each of them as their leader led a mini-liturgy of
patriotism, service, and farewell.

The group's leader read a tribute to "Comrade Budde," the title deliberately repeated at the start of each step of the litany of accolades and
accomplishments—Korean War-era veteran, elected official, husband and

1. Published originally as "Formation and the Custodians of Death," *Liturgy*, Vol.
20, No. 1 (January 2005). The Liturgical Conference, Inc. All rights reserved. Used by
permission.

father, and more. With a final salute to "Comrade Budde," the group of veterans marched out, some of whose uncooperative knees or joints were willed into a dignified compliance yet one more time.

I have had occasion to think of this military liturgy often in the past year. It has been hard not to, given the launching of new wars and commemoration of old ones following my father's death. I am struck by how very important the control of death—its presentation, its invocation, its commemoration—is to the ongoing legitimation of the American empire and the stories it tells about itself. These stories have a sacred quality to them, necessary to infuse the role of citizen with divine purpose and sanction sufficient to legitimate the body politic and the sacrifices demanded in its name.

Civil religion in its varied manifestations claims for itself the right to determine the meaning of death. Yet in so doing it collides with the Christian tradition—at least the self-aware and reflective aspects of the tradition—insofar as Christians claim that the meaning of death, and its purchase on present and future priorities and commitments, has been irrevocably and definitively claimed by the death and resurrection of Jesus. The interpretation of death held by Pilate and the early Church could not both be correct: no Caesar, past or present, may claim for Christians the meaning and power of death. As part of its birthright, the Church claims death as part of the ongoing process of making and delivering disciples, martyrs, and the communion of saints.

Yet the Church's stake in relating death to life and allegiance is all too easily obscured. My father's Mass of Christian Burial, while done with seriousness and respect, lacked something of the emphatic claims made to his life and death by his American Legion comrades. And despite the words of the liturgy, which dutifully connected death with baptism and resurrection, I suspect persons participating in both observances would have been persuaded that citizenship was the more powerful and formative category on display, eclipsing the more "private" role of being a lifelong Catholic Christian.

Ironically, both the Church and the state have a stake in how death is interpreted and internalized. Death has a formative role in making citizens and in making Christians, although in recent times state-centered control of death seems more intentional, systematic, and strategic. Churches have seemed content to affirm patriotic rituals even as their own practices regarding death become thinner, more therapeutic, and more thoroughly enfeebled as opportunities for building up the body of Christ.[2]

POLITICIZING THE DEAD

Governmental and media sources worked a curious transformation upon the nearly three thousand people killed on September 11, 2001. While the overwhelming majority of victims were civilians, in many ways all seemed to be accorded a status comparable to persons killed in combat. They did not just die, they died "for America"—as part of the American war against terrorism—even if relatively few were formally in service to America at the time (with the exception of many who died at the Pentagon).

Capitalism became even more closely tied with Americanism in commemorations for the dead at the World Trade Center. Inasmuch as terrorists attacked the towers as symbolic of American capitalism and economic might, the dead therein died nobly in the name of freedom— free mobility of capital, free trade in goods and services, free convertibility of currencies and various types of investment products.

The September 11 dead merited individualized eulogies and tributes in the established newspaper of record, as the New York Times ran biographies on every identified casualty. This individualized memorialization of "war-related" deaths—a distinctively modern practice mostly unknown in earlier times— worked both to sanctify the creed of individualism in American life while simultaneously bundling the deaths of each into a single package of nationalist outrage for which retribution seemed the only response capable of honoring the dead. Those families who spoke against retribution visited upon Afghanistan were marginalized and ignored, their individual attempts to reinterpret the meaning of their loved ones' deaths overwhelmed by the unifying commemorations that controlled the meaning of those deaths and that continue into the present.

In addition, September 11 produced a class of bona fide martyrs in service to America. New York City police and fire units, having lost hundreds of people in the line of duty, became overnight objects of veneration. Across the country, local and regional prayer services and public commemorations sought a representative of the New York police and fire departments. NYFD hats took on the qualities of sacramentals and holy

2. See Budde and Brimlow, *Christianity Incorporated*, chapter 4.

relics, and Mayor Rudy Guiliani for a time became the nation's new Moses; a calm, steady presence leading us through travails to the promised land of business-as-usual on the other side. Firefighters substituted for military heroes after September 11, and were valorized at sporting events, an important substitution given the limited ability of long-range bombing and ugly special-forces war in Afghanistan to produce properly sanitized icons capable of sustaining newly kindled patriotism and love of state.

Having rolled into and over (but as yet not out of) Afghanistan, the Bush administration sought to press the fallen heroes of September 11 into service justifying war against Iraq. Alongside fabricated claims of horrific weapons at the ready, the Bush administration repeatedly sought to link the noble sacrifice of American life on September 11 (it being noble to go to work) to the diabolical designs of Saddam Hussein.

As the campaign in Iraq has evolved from farcical mismatch to a war of attrition and occupation, the control of death's presentation remains central to state attempts to manage meaning and sacred devotion. The twin advances in bureaucratic personnel management and high-tech killing allow both for low U.S. casualties and the individual identification of those soldiers; no such precision is sought in counting and personifying the thousands of Iraqis killed, a continuation of Colin Powell's remark during the first Gulf War that the number of dead Iraqis was not a question he felt necessary to raise. As with September 11 casualties, each fallen soldier merits a reverential biography in the nation's newspapers, the full powers of journalistic human-interest writing focused on making the losses seem personal, the sacrifices even more poignant, with a select few (former NFL player Pat Tillman, for example) given a secular hagiography of privilege abandoned, asceticism embraced, and death assumed for the sake of others.

One can sometimes manage a glimpse at the larger imperatives when a momentary hitch causes the imperial management of death's presentation to stumble. Consider the official reaction to two such episodes in the past year: the unauthorized release of photos of a U.S. military mortuary, a room with several rows of caskets draped with American flags; and an episode of ABC's "Nightline" program, which read without comment the names of all U.S. personnel killed to date in the Iraq invasion and occupation. Ironically, in both cases, reactions dramatized the political nature of death management more than did the original events in question. The Bush administration criticized the coffin photos as an intrusion on family privacy, citing a Pentagon policy that claims that "the sensitivity and privacy of families of the fallen must be the first priority."[3] No one seemed to question how rows of anonymous coffins violated the privacy of any particular family, nor that such concerns seemed remote from the Pentagon's media relations officers who daily provided biographical information to reporters charged with writing patriotic tributes to the dead. No, what was at stake was something else: a specific anxiety that journalistic depictions of dead Americans in a deregulated fashion might undermine domestic support ("pictures of body bags from Vietnam" being the horrific of comparison in political circles), and a more general insistence that only the state—not the media, not the church, not anyone else—must be in control of death's presentation and management in our time. The latter anxiety, of death without a controlling political interpretation, comes through in the statement of Bush apologist Senator Lindsey Graham (R-SC), who defended banning the photos because "there is no ceremony held."[4] Without the narrative control of military commemoration, the meaning of death threatens to slip its harness and risks working at cross-purposes to those of state.

The April 30, 2004, episode of "Nightline" offered a forty-minute reading of the names (and display of pictures) of all Americans killed in the Iraq war (no names or pictures of Iraqi dead were offered). While the Bush administration official refrained from condemning the exercise, described by ABC News as "an expression of respect which simply seeks to honor those who have laid down their lives for their country," the Sinclair Broadcasting Group refused to air the program. Sinclair owns sixty-two television stations in thirty-nine markets, and claimed the program was an overt criticism of the war that risked undermining support for the conflict. Such an exercise "will have no proportionality" because it ignores other aspects of the U.S. war in Iraq, according to Sinclair vice-president Mark Hyman.[5]

In all of this, the control of death's presentation and meaning remains central to reinforcing the claims of modern citizenship above all other allegiances and identities. It also illustrates the extensive powers of death across time. Memorialization of those fallen in a noble cause can be

---

3. Chase, "Bush," 13.

4. Ibid.

5. Carter, "Some Stations."

used to legitimate contemporary killing and dying, even (or especially) in more morally ambiguous situations. In this respect, the completion of the official World War II Memorial comes as a godsend to the Bush regime as it struggles to consolidate its gains in Iraq.

Set on 7.4 acres of the mall in Washington DC, between the Washington Monument and the Lincoln Memorial, the formal dedication of the World War II Memorial on May 29, 2004, celebrated the heroism and patriotism of the "Good War" as the quintessence of American virtue. Like all official war monuments, the World War II Memorial is unambiguously a temple of civil religion. The most forthright expression of this comes from the USA Weekend magazine of April 30–May 2, 2004. This publication, an insert into hundreds of Sunday newspapers across the country, in addition to its usual celebrity news, recipes, and word puzzles, offered a lavish center article by Colin Powell on the World War II Memorial.[6] While emphasizing that war memorials "do not glorify war," he nonetheless highlighted their sacred status in affirming the ties of loyalty needed to prevail in war and peace.

Not content merely to reflect on how the new memorial honors those killed in combat sixty years ago, Powell put their sacrifice to work in affirming the contemporary martial needs of state: "Today, their descendants are fighting the global war against terrorism, serving and sacrificing in Afghanistan and Iraq and at other outposts on the front lines of freedom. The life of each and every one of them is precious to their loved ones and to our nation. And each life given in the name of liberty is a life that has not been lost in vain."[7]

In its design, the World War II Memorial was constructed as "a contemplative space" according to the *New York Times*.[8] It features a Rainbow Pool, with fountains between two arches that symbolize the European and Asian theaters of battle. On either side of the arches are fifty-four granite pillars, representing the American States, the District of Columbia, and nonstate American territories. Finally, visitors encounter a wall of four thousand gold stars, each representing one hundred Americans killed during the war. The intent is to represent national unity, "the country's spirit and sacrifice in the war, [and] the triumph of democracy."[9]

6. Powell, "Of Memory and Our Democracy," 8–9.

7. Ibid., 9.

8. Janofsky, "59 Years Later."

9. Ibid.

Not even this exercise in public sacralizing of war and death is sufficient for some nationalists. Conservative columnist Charles Krauthammer calls the World War II Monument's design a "disaster," complaining that it fails to inspire love of country over all amidst an array of misplaced symbols. He wonders why the monument pays tribute to the states and territories ("The Civil War was very much a war of states," he notes, but World War II was emphatically a national crusade). The "glory" of World War II, to Krauthammer, "was in its transcendence of geography—and class and ethnicity. Its fighting units mixed young men from every corner of America. Your classic World War II movie features the now-cliched platoon of the Polish millworker from Chicago, the Jewish kid from Brooklyn, the Appalachian woodsman and the Iowa farm boy bonding and fighting and dying for each other as a band of brothers." If the states—represented by granite pillars—are the wrong focus, "the ultimate banality" is the wall of four thousand gold stars, according to Krauthammer. Noting that gold stars were issued to families who lost a son in the war, Krauthammer assails the sheer arbitrariness of the number ("Why a hundred? Did they die in units of a hundred? Did they fight as centurions?"). "Four thousand stars are both too few and too many. Too few to represent the sheer mass, the unbearable weight of four hundred thousand dead. And too many—and too abstract—to represent the suffering of the mother of a single fallen hero."[10]

This sort of internal dispute, whatever else it does, highlights the perceived stakes in how death is controlled, presented, remembered, and enlisted for purposes of state. What is less obvious is that deaths claimed by and for America are (at least when the deceased are Christians) deaths taken from the beloved community of the Church, a down payment on allegiances needed for the next war instead of persons marching before us in the family of faith toward the promised kingdom of God.

CHRISTIANITY AND POLITICAL CONTROL OF DEATH

In retrospect, perhaps the single greatest failure of public policy implementation was Pilate's inability to secure the tomb of Jesus. He recognized the need to control the death of Jesus, even down to imposing the imperial seal on the tomb (the breaking of which constituted a criminal offense,

10. Krauthammer, "WWII Memorial a Lemon," 23.

hence making the resurrection a crime against the state), and dispatching a handful of soldiers to stand guard. Underestimating the personnel needs of a given job is a classic policy error, although given what happened (at least according to Christian accounts) dispatching the entire garrison might not have been enough.

The empty tomb represents the first—and by no means final—instance of Christ and his followers thwarting attempts to write death into a system-supporting script of state. Death on a cross, intended as a scandal and embarrassment, becomes a symbol of love conquering death; a sealed tomb intending to prove the empire's power to terminate a subversive story lived in a subversive fashion, instead becomes an unsealed doorway into the future, an ongoing story against which the greatest of powers have yet to prevail. Catacombs and coliseum, public executions and quiet, ordinary deaths—the church has sought to understand all of these as part of a longer, richer drama of allegiances and promises in which death is not the last word and sectarian political loyalties do not substitute for the universal body of Christ.

A full exposition of a proper Church-centered understanding of the dead and their role in the unfolding kingdom of God lies beyond this essay. At a minimum, however, a glimpse of a Christian appreciation of death and its role in the Church might help in understanding the significance of the state's attempt to roll death into the fabric of civil religion. One useful voice belongs to theologian Thomas G. Long, whose reminders on how Christians think about death and commemoration seem both timely and worthwhile. As he notes (in reference to tawdry, tacky trends in funerals explored by Jessica Mitford and others):

> Obviously, a genuine Christian funeral is not about the evils that Mitford found so easy to satirize—the vulgar, conspicuous consumption, the mawkish sentiment—but, strangely, a Christian funeral is also not primarily about many of the good things that its friends claim for it: the facilitation of grief, helping people to hold on to memories of the deceased, or even to supply pastoral care and comfort to the bereaved. A Christian funeral often provides these things, of course, but none of these is its central purpose. A Christian funeral is nothing less than a bold and dramatic worship of the living God done attentively to and in the face of an apparent victory at the hands of the last enemy. Though the liturgy may be gently worded, there is no hiding the fact that, in

a funeral, Christians raise a fist at death; recount the story of the Christ who suffered death, battled death, and triumphed over it; offer laments and thanksgiving to the God who raised Jesus from the grave; sing hymns of defiance; and honor the body and life of the saint who has died.[11]

Rather than being a place for the state to narrate the meaning of the deceased's life, or even for his family and friends to reminisce about his or her fine qualities, "the most important measure of a Christian funeral is its capacity to place the event of a person's death in the larger context of the Christian gospel. . . . The Christian funeral is a liturgical drama, a piece of gospel theater, with roles to play and a time honored, if flexible and culturally varied, script. . . . [T]hey are community enactments of a formative narrative."[12] Christian funeral rituals, properly understood, cannot be enlisted in the projects of empire; to the contrary, they can and should be opportunities of forming new disciples, of fashioning a continuity between the now-dead follower of Jesus and those on earth still on pilgrimage.

We have seen recently the coordinated powers of state funeral liturgy at their fullest in the weeklong, coast-to-coast adoration of Ronald Reagan (itself the product of a one hundred and thirty-plus page rubric administered by the armed forces). One would hope that some Christians would have noticed how utterly marginal and circumscribed were the distinctively ecclesial aspects of the Reagan events. The powers of state were on display, overwhelming matters religious (and remember, Reagan was a Christian, albeit a largely "unchurched" one) with a nationalist narration unrestrained in its self-exultation and overt in its desire to shape hearts and dispositions.

When Christians take more seriously the formative powers—for the living, on The Way—of ecclesial death practices and the power attendant to telling the story properly, perhaps they will be less willing to hand their dead over to managers and architects of civil religion and love of state. The latter will not willingly surrender so powerful a set of associations in our culture. Yet if and when the liberation of Christian death from the hands of empire arrives, perhaps the dead may rest in peace with our Lord instead of being conscripted into the next war on earth.

11. T. Long, "Why Jessica Mitford Was Wrong," 503.

12. Ibid., 507–8.

Bibliography

Allen, John L., Jr. "The Deathbed Friendship between a Bishop and an Atheist." *National Catholic Reporter.* August 24, 2007. http://ncronline.org/blogs/all-things-catholic/deathbed-friendship-between-bishop-and-atheist.

———. "Torture in His History Taints Spanish Martyr's Beatification." *National Catholic Reporter,* October 12, 2007. http://ncronline.org/blogs/all-things-catholic/torture-his-history-taints-spanish-martyrs-beatification.

Aspen Institute. *Where Will They Lead? MBA Student Attitudes about Business and Society.* Aspen: Aspen Institute, 2001.

Associated Press. "Polish Church Reports Secret Police Ties." June 27, 2007.

———. "Warsaw Archbishop says he Leaves his Fate with Pope amid Scandal over Communist Collaboration." January 5, 2007.

Barrett, David B., and Todd M. Johnson. "Annual Statistical Table on Global Mission: 2004." *International Bulletin of Mission Research* 28 (2004) 24–25.

Barrionuevo, Alexei. "Argentine Church faces 'Dirty War' Past." *New York Times,* September 17, 2007. http://www.nytimes.com/2007/09/17/world/americas/17church.html.

Bell, Derrick A. *Faces at the Bottom of the Well: The Permanence of Racism.* New York: Basic, 1992.

"Benedict XVI: Religion No Threat to Nation's Unity." *CBCP News,* June 28, 2009. http://www.cbcpnews.com/?q=node/9406

Brimlow, Robert. "Paganism and the Professions." Edited by D. Stephen Long. Renewing Radical Discipleship Pamphlet 3. The Ekklesia Project, 2002. http://www.ekklesiaproject.org.

Brunner, Emil. *The Misunderstanding of the Church.* Translated by Harold Knight. Philadelphia: Westminster, 1952.

Budde, Michael L. "God is Not a Capitalist." In *God is Not,* edited by D. Brent Laytham. Grand Rapids: Brazos, 2003.

———. *The (Magic) Kingdom of God: Christianity and Global Culture Industries.* Boulder: Westview, 1997.

———. "Selling America, Restricting the Church." In *Anxious About Empire: Theological Essays on the New Global Realities,* edited by Wesley Avram. Grand Rapids: Brazos, 2004.

Budde, Michael L., and Robert Brimlow. *Christianity Incorporated: How Big Business is Buying the Church.* Grand Rapids: Brazos, 2002.

Buell, Denise Kimber. *Why This New Race: Ethnic Reasoning in Early Christianity.* New York: Columbia University Press, 2005.

Bibliography

Burke, Hilary. "Argentine Priest Conviction Puts Church in Hot Seat." *Reuters*, October 10, 2007. http://www.reuters.com/article/2007/10/10/idUSN10275964.

Bush, George W. Introduction to National Security Statement, September 17, 2002.

Carothers, Thomas, and William Barndt. "Civil Society." *Foreign Policy* 117 (1999/2000) 18–24, 26–29.

Carter, Bill. "Some Stations to Block 'Nightline' War Tribute." *New York Times*, April 30, 2004.

Catholic News Agency. "To Be a Good Christian Is to Be a Good Citizen, Explains the Holy Father." *Catholic News Agency*, October 31, 2007.

Cavanaugh, William T. "Killing for the Telephone Company: Why the Nation-State is Not the Keeper of the Common Good." *Modern Theology* 20 (2004) 243–74.

———. *The Myth of Religious Violence*. Oxford: Oxford University Press, 2009.

Center for the Study of Church Management. Online: http://www.villanova. edu/business/excellence/churchmgmt/

Cesarani, David, and Mary Fulbrook. *Citizenship, Nationality and Migration in Europe*. New York: Routledge, 1996.

Chase, Randall. "Bush: Privacy of Coffin Photos First Priority." *Chicago Tribune*, April 24, 2004, 13.

Claiborne, Shane, and Chris Haw. *Jesus for President: Politics for Ordinary Radicals*. Designed by SharpSeven. Grand Rapids: Zonvervan, 2008.

Coleman, John A. "Globalization and Catholic Social Thought: Mutual Challenges." In *Christian Political Ethics*, edited by John A. Coleman, 170–89. Washington, DC: Georgetown University Press, 2008.

Collins, Denis. "The Voluntary Brainwashing of Humanities Students in Stanford's MBA Program: Student Complaints and Some Recommendations." *Business Ethics Quarterly* 6 (1996) 393–413.

Conant, Eve, and Richard Wolfe. "Obama's New Gospel." *Newsweek*, May 3, 2008. http://www.newsweek.com/2008/05/03/obama-s-new-gospel.html.

Congregation for the Doctrine of the Faith. "Letter to the Bishops of the Catholic Church on Some Aspects of the Church Understood as Communion." 1992. http://www.vatican.va/roman_curia/congregations/cfaith/documents/rc_con_cfaith_doc_28051992_communionis-notio_en.html.

Curanovic, Alicja. "The Attitudes of the Moscow Patriarchate towards Other Orthodox Churches." *Religion, State & Society* 35 (2007) 301–18.

Del Colle, Ralph. "The Pursuit of Holiness: A Roman Catholic-Pentecostal Dialogue." *Journal of Ecumenical Studies* 37 (2000) 301–20.

Della Cava, Ralph. "Transnational Religions: The Roman Catholic Church in Brazil and the Orthodox Church in Russia." *Sociology of Religion*, 62 (2001) 535–50.

DeYoung, Curtiss Paul, Michael O. Emerson, George Yancey, and Karen Chai Kim. "All Churches Should Be Multiracial: The Biblical Case." *Christianity Today*, April 1, 2005. http://www.christianitytoday.com/ct/2005/april/22.33.html.

Dolbee, Sandee, and Mark Sauer. "Report Shows Diocese's Accounting System Lacking." *San Diego Union-Tribune*, July 31, 2007.

Drucker, Peter. *Managing the Nonprofit Organization: Practices and Principles*. New York: HarperCollins, 1990.

Ellul, Jacques. *Propaganda: The Formation of Men's Attitudes*. New York: Vintage, 1973.

Emerson, Michael, with Rodney Woo. *People of the Dream: Multiracial Congregations in America*. Princeton: Princeton University Press, 2006.

Everist, Norma Cook. "The Burning of Black Churches and the Ecclesiology of American Civil Religion." *Currents in Theology and Mission* 24 (1997) 336–47.

Federation for American Immigration Reform (FAIR). "The Morality of Mass Immigration from a Roman Catholic Perspective." 2006. http://www.fairus.org/site/PageServer?pagename=research_immigration_morality

Fallaci, Oriana. *The Force of Reason.* New York: Rizzoli International, 2004.

Frank, R. H., T. D. Gilovich, and D. T. Regan, "Does Studying Economics Inhibit Cooperation?" *Journal of Economic Perspectives* 7 (1993) 159–71.

Fulkerson, Mary McClintock. "A Place to Appear: Ecclesiology as if Bodies Mattered." *Theology Today* 64 (2007) 159–71.

George, Sherron K. "Brazil: An 'Evangelized' Giant Calling for Liberating Evangelism." *International Bulletin of Missionary Research* 26:3 (2002) 104–9.

Ghoshal, Sumantra. "Bad Management Theories are Destroying Good Management Practices." *Academy of Management Learning and Education* 4:1 (2005) 75–91.

Gluck, Frederick W. "Can the Church Learn from Wal-Mart?" *America* 190:17 (2004). http://www.americamagazine.org/content/article.cfm?article_id=3598

———. "Crisis Management in the Church." *America* 189:18 (2002). http://www.americamagazine.org/content/article.cfm?article_id=3310

Gregory, Brad. *Salvation at Stake: Christian Martyrs in Early Modern Europe.* Cambridge: Harvard University Press, 1999.

Hastings, Adrian. "Christianity and Nationhood: Congruity or Antipathy?" *Journal of Religious History* 25:3 (2001) 247–60.

Haughey, John C. "Affections and Business, Proceedings of the Second National Consultation on Corporate Ethics." Center for Ethics and Corporate Policy, Chicago, May 13–15, 1978.

Hays, Richard. *The Moral Vision of the New Testament: A Contemporary Introduction to New Testament Ethics.* San Francisco: HarperSanFrancisco, 1996.

Hessert, Paul. "Theology and Money." *Explor* 4:2 (1978) 21–32.

Hollenbach, David. "The Life of the Human Community." *America* 167:14 (2002) 6–8.

Hovey, Craig. *To Share in the Body: A Theology of Martyrdom for Today's Church.* Grand Rapids: Brazos, 2008.

Hundley, Tom. "Tortured Priest's Tenacity Exposes Betrayal in Church." *Chicago Tribune*, February 26, 2007. http://articles.chicagotribune.com/2007-02-26/news/0702260135_1_fellow-priests-files-virgin-mary.

Huntington, Samuel. *The Clash of Civilizations and the Remaking of World Order.* New York: Simon & Schuster, 1998.

———. *Who Are We? The Challenges to American National Identity.* New York: Simon & Schuster, 2004.

Janofsky, Michael. "59 Years Later, Memorial to World War II Veterans Opens on Mall." *New York Times*, April 30, 2004.

Jeffrey, Paul. "After 25 Years, 'St. Romero of the World' Still Inspires." *National Catholic Reporter*, April 15, 2005. http://findarticles.com/p/articles/mi_m1141/is_24_41/ai_n13675633/

Jenkins, Philip. *The Next Christendom.* New York: Oxford University Press, 2002.

John Paul II. "Ecclesia in America: Post-Synodal Apostolic Exhortation." 1999. Online: http://www.vatican.va/holy_father/john_paul_ii/apost_exhortations/documents/hf_jp-ii_exh_22011999_ecclesia-in-america_en.html.

Bibliography

Johnson, Chalmers. *The Sorrows of Empire: Militarism, Secrecy, and the End of the Republic*. New York: Metropolitan, 2004.

Kennedy, D. James, with Jerry Newcombe. *How Would Jesus Vote? A Christian Perspective on the Issues*. New York: Waterbrook, 2008.

Kishkovsky, Sophia. "Conflict Tests Ties Between the Georgian and Russian Orthodox Churches." *New York Times*, September 6, 2008. http://www.nytimes .com/2008/09/06/world/europe/06orthodox.html.

Krauthammer, Charles. "WWII Memorial a Lemon." *Chicago Tribune*, May 31, 2004, 23.

Kravl, Chris, and Tracy Wilkinson. "Assassinated Archbishop to Join Beatification Path." *Los Angeles Times*, March 30, 2005. http://wwrn.org/ articles/16181/?&place=central-america&section=christianity.

Kreider, Alan. "Violence and Mission in the Fourth and Fifth Centuries: Lessons for Today." *International Bulletin for Mission Research* 31:3 (2007) 125–33.

Kress, Robert. "The Priest-Pastor as CEO." *America* 186.8 (2002). http://www.america-magazine.org/content/article.cfm?article_id=1629.

Kung, Hans, and Karl-Joseph Kuschel. *A Global Ethic: The Declaration of the Parliament of the World's Religions*. New York: Continuum, 1993.

Laufer, Peter. *Wetback Nation*. Chicago: Ivan Dee, 2004.

Letter to Diognetus. http://www.ccel.org/ccel/richardson/fathers.x.i.ii.html.

Levitske, Brooke. "Illegal Immigration and the Church: Philanthropic Lawlessness." *Acton Institute Commentary*, July 11, 2007. http://www.acton.org/pub/commentary/2007/07/11/illegal-immigration-and-church-philanthropic-lawlessness.

Levitt, Peggy. *God Needs No Passport: Immigrants and the Changing American Religious Landscape*. New York: New Press, 2007.

Lewis, Ted, editor. *Electing Not to Vote*. Eugene, OR: Cascade, 2008.

Lohfink, Gerhard. *Jesus and Community*. Philadelphia: Fortress, 1984.

Long, D. Stephen. *Speaking of God: Theology, Language, and Truth*. Grand Rapids: Eerdmans, 2009.

Long, Thomas G. "Why Jessica Mitford Was Wrong." *Theology Today* 55 (1999) 496–509.

Dobbs, Lou. "Lou Dobbs Tonight Transcripts." 2006. http://archives.cnn.com/ TRANSCRIPTS/0601/18/ldt.01.html January 18.

Luxmoore, Jonathan. "The Secret Policemen's Bishop." *The Tablet*, January 13, 2007. http:// www.thetablet.co.uk/article/9195.

———. "Tinker, Tailor, Soldier, Priest." *The Table*, August 12, 2006. http://www.thetablet. co.uk/article/8431.

Mandaville, Peter. *Transnational Muslim Politics: Reimagining the Umma*. New York: Routledge, 2004.

March, Andrew. "The Demands of Citizenship: Translating Political Liberalism into the Language of Islam." *Journal of Muslim Minority Affairs* 25:3 (2005) 317–45.

Marx, Anthony. *Faith in Nation: Exclusionary Origins of Nationalism*. Oxford: Oxford University Press, 2003.

Maxwell, William W. "Race and Religion: The Elixir of Separation." *CrossCurrents* (Summer 2007) 150–55.

MacIntyre, Alasdair. *After Virtue: A Study in Moral Theory*. South Bend, IN: University of Notre Dame Press, 1981.

Martinez, Javier. "Beyond Secular Reason: Some Contemporary Challenges for the Life and Thought of the Church." *Communio* 31 (2004) 557–86.

McCann Dennis P., and M. L. Brownsburger. "Management as a Social Practice: Rethinking Business Ethics after MacIntyre." *Annual of the Society of Christian Ethics* (1990) 223–45.

McCarraher, Eugene. "The False Gospel of Work: Against the Cant of Diligence and Virtue." *Books and Culture* 12:4 (July 2006) 26.

———. "Money Is the Root of All Order: Corporate Humanism as Domestic Containment, 1945–1965." Unpublished manuscript, n.d.

———. "Smile When You Say 'Laity': The Hidden Triumph of the Consumer Ethos." *Commonweal*, September 12, 1997. Online: http://findarticles.com/p/articles/mi_m1252/is_15_124/ai_58400716/

McDermott, Jeremy. "'Interrogator in a Cassock' Given Life." *The Scotsman*, October 11, 2007.

Mignone, Emilio. *Witness to the Truth: The Complicity of Church and Dictatorship in Argentina.* Maryknoll, NY: Orbis, 1988.

Mikulich, Alex. "Mapping 'Whiteness': The Complexity of Racial Formation and the Subversive Moral Imagination of the 'Motley Crowd.'" *Journal of the Society of Christian Ethics* 25:1 (2005) 99–122.

Milbank, John. *Theology and Social Theory: Beyond Secular Reason.* London: Blackwell, 1990.

Neuhaus, Richard John. "Checks, Balances, and Bishops." *First Things* (September 2006). http://www.firstthings.com/article/2009/03/checks-balances-and-bishops-31.

Novak, Michael. *The Spirit of Democratic Capitalism.* New York: Simon & Schuster, 1982.

Obama, Barack. "Obama's Remarks on Wright." *New York Times*, April 29, 2008. http://www.nytimes.com/2008/04/29/us/politics/29text-obama.html?pagewanted=all.

O'Donovan, Oliver. *The Just War Revisited.* Current Issues in Theology 2. Cambridge: Cambridge University Press, 2003.

Ovodal, Ralph. "Romanizing America Through Illegal Immigration." 2006. http://www.pccmonroe.org/Ecumenism/romanizingamerica.htm.

Pabst, Adrian. "Kirill Is not the Kremlin's Man." *The Guardian*, July 28, 2009. http://www.guardian.co.uk/commentisfree/belief/2009/jul/28/kirill-ukraine-russia-orthodox

Paeth, Scott. "Shared Values in Communal Life: Provisional Skepticism and the Prospect of a Global Ethic." *Journal of Ecumenical Studies* 42 (2007) 407–24.

Pfeffer, Jeffrey. "Why Do Bad Management Theories Persist? A Comment on Ghoshal." *Academy of Management Learning & Education* 4 (2005) 96–100.

Powell, Colin. "Of Memory and Our Democracy." *USA Weekend*, April 30–May 2, 2004, 8–9.

Rasmussen, Arne. "Ecclesiology and Ethics: The Difficulties of Ecclesial Moral Reflection." *Ecumenical Review* 52:2 (2000) 180–94.

Robert, Dana. "Shifting Southward: Global Christianity Since 1945." *International Bulletin of Missionary Research* 24:2 (2000) 50–58.

Roberts, Donald F., et al. "Kids and Media at the New Millennium: A Kaiser Family Foundation Report." San Francisco, CA: Kaiser Family Foundation, 1999.

Roediger, David. *Working Toward Whiteness: How America's Immigrants Became White.* New York: Basic, 2005.

Roudometof, Victor. "Greek Orthodoxy, Territoriality, and Globality: Religious Responses and Institutional Disputes." *Sociology of Religion* 69:1 (2008) 67–91.

Roy, Olivier. *Globalized Islam: The Search for a New Ummah.* New York: Columbia University Press, 2004.

Bibliography

Salisbury, Joyce. *The Blood of Martyrs: Unintended Consequences of Ancient Violence*. New York: Routledge, 2004.

Sanneh, Lamin. *Whose Religion Is Christianity? The Gospel Beyond the West*. Grand Rapids: Eerdmans, 2003.

Schmidt, Garbi. "The Transnational Umma: Myth or Reality? Examples from the Western Diasporas." *Muslim World* 95 (October 2005) 575–86.

Schwarz, Ludwig, and Manfred Scheuer. "Forward." In Erna Putz, *Franz Jagerstatter: A Shining Example in Dark Times*. Linz, Austria: Diocese of Linz, 2007. http://www.dioezese-linz.at/redaktion/index.php?action_new=Lesen&Article_ID=39496.

Sharp, Douglas. "Evangelicals, Racism, and the Limits of Social Science Research." *Christian Scholars Review* 33 (2004) 237–61.

Shenk, Wilbert. "Recasting Theology of Mission: Impulses from the Non-Western World." *International Bulletin of Missionary Research* 25:3 (2001) 98–107.

Slattery, Joseph. *The Suffering Faces of the Poor Are the Suffering Faces of Christ*. Tulsa, OK: Diocese of Tulsa, 2007.

Smith, Christian, with Melinda Lundquist Denton. *Soul Searching: The Religious and Spiritual Lives of American Teenagers*. New York: Oxford University Press, 2005.

Smith, Craig. "Ties to Communist Secret Police Snare Polish Bishop." *New York Times*, January 6, 2007. http://www.nytimes.com/2007/01/06/world/europe/06poland.html?ref=stanislawwielgus

Smith, Gregory. "Attitudes Toward Immigration: In the Pulpit and the Pew." *Pew Forum on Religion and Public Life*, April 26, 2006. http://pewresearch.org/pubs/20/attitudes-toward-immigration-in-the-pulpit-and-the-pew

Smith, Lacey Baldwin. *Fools, Martyrs, Traitors: The Story of Martyrdom in the Western World*. New York: Knopf, 1997.

Stackhouse, Max. "Civil Religion, Political Theology and Public Theology: What's the Difference?" *Political Theology* 5 (2004) 275–93.

———. "General Introduction." In *God and Globalization, Volume I: Religion and the Powers of the Common Life*, edited by Max Stackhouse and Peter Paris, 1–51. Harrisburg, PA: Trinity, 2000.

Stafford, Tim. "The Business of the Kingdom." *Christianity Today*, November 19, 1999. http://www.ctlibrary.com/ct/1999/november15/9td042.html.

Stewart, I. C. "Accounting and Accountability: Double Entry, Double Nature, Double Identity." *Crux* 26:2 (1990). http://www.redcliffe.org/uploads/documents/dancing_with_elephants2_10.pdf

Swidler, Leonard. *After the Absolute: The Dialogical Future of Religious Reflection*. Minneapolis: Fortress, 1990.

———. "Toward a Universal Declaration of a Global Ethic." *Journal of Ecumenical Studies* 42:3 (2007). http://globalethic.org/Center/intro.htm.

Twitchell, James B. "Jesus Christ Superflock." *Mother Jones* 30:2 (2005) 46–49.

United States Conference of Catholic Bishops. *Forming Consciences for Faithful Citizenship*. Washington, DC: USCCB, 2007.

Usborne, David. "Argentina's Disappeared." *The Independent*, October 11, 2007.

Van Gelder, Craig. "Rethinking Denominations and Denominationalism in Light of a Missional Ecclesiology." *Word & World* 25 (2005) 23–33.

Waalkes, Scott. *The Fullness of Time in a Flat World: Globalization and the Liturgical Year*. Theopolitical Visions 6. Eugene, OR: Cascade, 2010.

Wallis, Jim. *The Great Awakening: Reviving Faith and Politics in a Post-Religious Right America*. New York: HarperOne, 2008.

Walls, Andrew. *The Cross-Cultural Process in Christian History*. Maryknoll, NY: Orbis, 2002.

———. "Eusebius Tries Again: Reconceiving the Study of Christian History." *International Bulletin of Missionary Research* 24:3 (2000) 105–25.

———. *The Missionary Movement in Christian History: Studies in the Transmission of Faith*. Maryknoll, NY: Orbis, 1996.

———. "Toward a Global Church History." *International Bulletin of Missionary Research* 20 (1996) 50–57.

Watkins, Clare. "The Church as a 'Special' Case: Comments from Ecclesiology Concerning the Management of the Church." *Modern Theology* 9 (1993) 369–84.

West, Robert W., and Charles Zech. "Internal Financial Controls in the U.S. Catholic Church." Online: http://www.villanova.edu/business/assets/documents/excellence/church/catholicchurchfinances.pdf.

Wilmore, Gayraud. "Struggling Against Racism With Realism and Hope." *Journal for Preachers* 29:2 (2000) 29–35.

Winfield, Nicole. "Religion in the News." *Associated Press*, August 3, 2007. http://wwrn.org/articles/25819/?&place=vatican.

Wright, Jeremiah. "The African-American Religious Experience." *National Press Club*, April 28, 2008. http://www.chicagotribune.com/news/politics/chi-wright transcript-04282008,0,3113697.story.

Wuthnow, Robert. *Boundless Faith: The Global Outreach of American Churches*. Berkeley: University of California Press, 2009.

Wuthnow, Robert, and Stephen Offutt. "Transnational Religious Connections." *Sociology of Religion* 69:2 (2008) 209–32.

Yoder, John Howard. *The Priestly Kingdom: Social Ethics as Gospel*. Notre Dame, IN: University of Notre Dame Press, 1986.

Zahn, Gordon. *In Solitary Witness: The Life and Death of Franz Jägerstätter*. Springfield, IL: Templegate, 1964.